TELLING STORIES

wishing you good stories
and happy endings!

Toy Cartlidge

Smyth & Helwys Publishing, Inc.
6316 Peake Road
Macon, Georgia 31210-3960
1-800-747-3016

The paper used in this publication meets the minimum requirements of
American National Standard for Information Sciences—
Permanence of Paper for Printed Library Materials.
ANSI Z39.48–1984. (alk. paper)

Library of Congress Cataloging-in-Publication Data

Cartledge, Tony W.
Telling stories : tall tales and deep truths / by Tony Cartledge.
p. cm.
Includes index.
ISBN 978-1-57312-515-4 (alk. paper)
1. Bible--Criticism, interpretation, etc.
2. Bible stories, English. I.
Title.
BS511.3.C39 2008
242'.5--dc22
2008016552

TELLING STORIES

TALL TALES & DEEP TRUTHS

TONY CARTLEDGE

DEDICATION

For my parents, William and Hollie Cartledge, who have lived out stories of plain truth and simple goodness, stories that shaped my values, taught me much, and continue to inspire. My own love of storytelling owes no small debt to memories of my mother "doing the voices" of Brer Rabbit and company as she entertained three boys with Uncle Remus stories, and I am grateful.

ACKNOWLEDGMENTS

Paul C. Reviere, Jr., my boyhood friend, taught me how to ride a horse and to make a toy-sized funeral spray from a zinnia blossom and three toothpicks. Paul's youthful imagination inspired my own, and his adult career as pastor, teacher, coroner, funeral director, and shag instructor (concurrently) continues to earn my admiration.

The five churches that were gracious enough to call me as their pastor are worthy of praise, if not sympathy. They are Loco Baptist Church in Lincolnton, Georgia (a story in itself); Highland Baptist Church in Hogansville, Georgia; Tabbs Creek Baptist Church in Oxford, North Carolina; Oak Grove Baptist Church in Boone, North Carolina; and Woodhaven Baptist Church near Apex, North Carolina. The good people of those churches suffered through many poor sermons and a few good ones; their feedback enriched and improved my preaching along the way. I'm particularly grateful to those who were prone to say, "You ought to put those stories into a book."

My students at Campbell University Divinity School, especially those who are brave enough to sign up for my "Ministry of Writing" classes, continue to earn my gratitude. They keep me on my toes.

As always, I am immensely grateful to my wife, Jan, who has a keen eye for pointing out my typographical errors, and a gracious spirit that refrains from drawing excessive attention to my other faults.

TABLE OF CONTENTS

PREFACE

It is no secret that stories are integral to the human experience. As soon as language took hold of the human imagination, stories emerged to pass on the traditions and understandings that give meaning to life. Family, cultural, political, and religious systems—consciously or not—employ stories to inform, to explain, to inspire, to indoctrinate. In so doing, a common inventory of stories contributes to a common sense of identity.

Social scientists have long recognized the power of stories. Anthropologists analyze peoples of the past and take careful note of the legends that have persevered from ancient days, comparing them across cultures and continents and confirming their ongoing influence. Contemporary observers note that postmodern people put a priority on relationships with others and the stories in which they live.

For Christians, the Bible is our story *par excellence*, a collection of many different stories that unite within one overarching story that tells us who we are and why we are here and where we are going. The Bible contains stories of origins and history, stories of warning and woe, stories of triumph and hope. It contains poetry and narrative, hair-raising tales and mind-numbing lists, vicarious forays into hoary histories and apocalyptic futures. Together, these stories become the story of a people who were led by the Spirit of God to worship the One revealed in the Old Testament through Yahweh and in the New Testament through Jesus. The Bible is *one story* made of *many stories* that declare *God's story*—as understood by the humans who believe God has been revealed to them in many and various ways.

For those who long to understand the truths found in Scripture—and those who are charged with explaining them—stories remain primary windows into the biblical text. The best preachers are often the best storytellers, and there is no better model than Jesus, who rarely made a point without telling a story.

If the Gospel accounts are an accurate guide, Jesus' preaching most commonly began with stories, rather than with a text. Luke's account of Jesus' first sermon (Luke 4:16-30) appears to be an exception, though he was only following custom when he visited the synagogue in Nazareth and read a Scripture text before sitting down to teach. On that day, the chosen Scripture was from Isaiah 61, a text widely interpreted as a description of a future Messiah.

After reading the text, Jesus sat down to teach, but all we are told of his sermon is this: "Today this scripture has been fulfilled in your hearing" (v. 21). That alone was enough to cause such a stir that the religious leaders threw him out of the synagogue and tried to cast him from a cliff.

In the extended discourse we remember as the "Sermon on the Mount" (Matthew 5–7), Jesus gave instructions that occasionally referenced Hebrew Scriptures or traditions, usually in order to proclaim a higher standard, but his teaching was also laced with metaphors and elements of stories.

The teachings that most of us remember best are the ones we call "parables," stories Jesus told to make a point. The stories appear to have been original creations that sprang from Jesus' imagination and usually required little commentary. It is clear that Jesus intended to make people think, and he often told stories that raised crucial questions, then left them open-ended.

Did the prodigal son's older brother ever heed his father's plea to join the welcome-home party for his repentant sibling (Luke 15:11-32), or did he maintain the self-righteous and unforgiving spirit that left him on the outside of grace? We don't know. Did the fruitless fig tree that was first condemned but then fertilized with manure and given a second chance (Luke 13:6-9) ever produce any fruit? We don't know.

We don't know, because stories like those were not about elder brothers or fig trees: they were about the men and women and children who listened to Jesus' stories—or who read and ponder them today. Jesus knew the power of a story to set minds in motion and raise questions that might otherwise remain dormant.

Jesus was not the first biblical personage to employ engaging stories for dynamic effect. When the prophet Nathan set out to confront King David regarding his adulterous and murderous behavior toward Bathsheba and her husband Uriah, he could have begun by quoting the commandments against murder, adultery, stealing, and coveting one's neighbor's wife (Exod 20:13-15, 17), because David had broken all of them. He did not begin his sermon with a text, however, for the king would immediately have raised his defenses and might have refused to hear the prophetic word. Instead, Nathan told the king a heart-rending story about an unfeeling tycoon who stole his poor neighbor's beloved lamb (2 Sam 12:1-4). Nathan's unvarnished story touched David's heart and set the stage for the fallen king to become deeply convicted of his personal sin and need for repentance.

When Isaiah of Jerusalem sought to help ordinary Israelites understand why their sin had put them on a path to national dissolution, he could have quoted from the Deuteronomistic tradition and warned them outright of their coming doom. Instead, he sang them a song that told a story about a faithful farmer who prepared and cultivated a vineyard with extraordinary efforts, choice plants, tender care, and round-the-clock protection (Isa 5:1-7). The hardworking landowner longed to taste the fruit of his labors, but his carefully tended vines produced only worthless, noxious grapes. The people, no doubt, would have immediately sympathized with the farmer's decision to cease caring for the thankless vineyard and leave it to be overrun with briers and thorns. When the prophet concluded, "For the vineyard of the LORD of hosts is the house of Israel and the people of Judah are his pleasant planting," they got the point.

So it was that Jesus built upon the prophetic storytelling tradition by creating a plethora of parables that served to catch his hearers' attention, set the wheels of their minds in motion, and prepare their hearts for a word from God.

In telling stories, Jesus often used imagination and metaphor, pulling attention-grabbing stories and images from the air. He asked his hearers to imagine someone who could examine a speck in another's eye while a plank protruded from his own, or to visualize a great camel squeezing through the eye of a needle. He spoke of a despised Samaritan who showed unexpected compassion and a bigger-barn-building landowner who thought only of himself.

Jesus' hearers understood that the characters and events in those memorable stories didn't have to be real in order for the stories to be true.

In my preaching experience of nearly forty years, I have often resorted to the telling of creative stories as an avenue for capturing the attention and engaging the minds of those who found themselves listening to the message I was called upon to bring. I cannot say if those were the best sermons I have ever preached, but I can testify that the ones people remember best and request most are those that begin with something along the order of "Once upon a time . . . ."

The following chapters contain a smorgasbord of stories and scripts that range from the possible to the fantastic, along with one that really happened. They include original stories in folktale style, and monologues or dialogues designed to illuminate biblical characters. All of the stories were written with a text in mind, and sometimes the text is incorporated into the story. Most often, however, the story stands alone and serves the role of an interactive plow designed to stir the imagination and prepare the hearts of listeners to be more receptive to the scriptural seeds that follow.

In one way or another, the story-sermons found here fall into the realm of what is generally called "narrative preaching," though the term defies precise definition and can suggest everything from relating the Scripture as a story to telling stories about the Scripture. They were not written with any thought to following a particular model, however, but simply reflect an intuitive attempt to communicate biblical truth in appealing ways.

It is my hope that the following stories may prove to be worthwhile reading for all thoughtful persons, and may inspire those who proclaim Christ to effectively utilize good stories in their own preaching.

Unless otherwise noted, Scripture quotations are from the
New Revised Standard Version.

Part 1
IT COULD HAPPEN

THE HOUSE WHERE GOODNESS DWELLS

2 Peter 3:8-15a

Rosemary Evans was a redheaded stepchild, and that's just the way it was. Her wavy hair was the color of bright rust, like the streaks running down the tin roof of her grandfather's workshop. It stayed long most of the time, not because she wanted it that way but because her mother Mitzi could trim the dead ends occasionally without having to spend either money or time taking Rosie to the beauty shop.

Mitzi's first husband had been a soldier. He shipped out for Iraq less than a month after his daughter was born, and the Army shipped him back in a box with a flag on the top. Rosie had seen the pictures; she knew. On her dresser she kept a framed picture of a smiling man with a buzz cut who held a tiny baby and looked at her with obvious wonder. She didn't remember having the picture made, of course, but she knew that the tender joy in his eyes was for her.

Rosie didn't see any of that tenderness in her stepfather. He was a military man, too, and he came back from the war with his body intact, but something had been damaged on the inside. Emotional explosions must have scarred his heart, Rosie thought, and left him angry. He tried to be a good man, but it was hard for him. He doctored his pain with beer and booze he bought at the store and with little bags of crystal methamphetamine he bought from a man named

Skeeter. Sometimes he could be almost nice, but most of the time, Rosie was afraid of him.

She was a little bit afraid of her mother, too. Rosie had been three years old when Dan Saggit moved in, and six when he and her mother finally married. She couldn't understand why her mother needed anyone other than her. Nor could Rosie understand why her mother liked getting drunk or stoned with Dan, or why sometimes they would go out and leave her at home alone. Dan had never shown much love toward Rosie, and Mitzi often acted as if the girl with her father's red hair was an inconvenience. Children notice things like that.

Rosie's saving grace was her Grandpa Jim Evans, who had lost his son but was determined not to let his granddaughter go. He and Grandma June would take care of Rosie when Mitzi and Dan went on vacations by themselves, and they could come and pick her up if she was left alone at night and got scared. On Sunday mornings, they always came by for Rosie and took her to church with them, even when they had to come inside and help her get dressed because Mitzi and Dan were still sleeping. After a while, they just started inviting Rosie to spend the weekends with them, and her parents were happy for the greater freedom.

When she went to her grandparents' home, Rosie felt as if goodness and love simply seeped from the walls and washed over her. She delighted in being there, and she determined that she wanted to be good like her grandparents were good, that she wanted to love people the way God and Jesus did, the way they talked about in Sunday school.

Mitzi held a sort of grudging respect for her former in-laws. A part of her resented their continuing involvement in her life. But another part recognized that Rosie needed someone to love her unconditionally. Which part came to the surface changed with her moods and her state of sobriety. Dan didn't really care if Rosie's grandparents paid her extra attention, so long as he didn't have to do it.

When Rosie was eight years old, Grandpa Jim offered to build her a playhouse in the back yard. "Actually, Rosie, it'll be more than a playhouse," he said. "I'll make it big enough and nice enough so that you can play in it now, but when you're older, you can make it into an art studio, or a music room, or whatever you want it to be. It will be your special place."

Rosie squealed with glee as she flung her arms around Grandpa Jim's neck and didn't even mind the way his scruffy whiskers scratched her cheek. "Oh, Grandpa," she said, "that would be the nicest thing anyone has ever done for me. And I promise that I will take good care of it and it will be a good house. I won't let any bad people or bad things inside. It will always be a place like your house, Grandpa, a place where goodness is at home."

Grandpa Jim had cleared the project with Mitzi and Dan, and he soon set to work in a corner of the backyard. He brought truckloads of lumber, and set up his table saw, and called on a friend from church to help him with the big floor joists and with framing the walls and raising the rafters. He put siding on the outside that was painted white to match the house, and there was a window on each side of the door with picket shutters that he painted Christmas tree green because that was Rosie's favorite color.

There were windows on the other walls, too, and Grandpa Jim even put two skylights in the roof because he said a house could never have too much light in it. He finished the walls and the ceilings just like in a regular house, and he let Rosie pick out the pale green paint for the walls. The color was called "Sea Foam," and Rosie admired the way it blended with the sand-colored carpet.

Grandpa's church friend helped him bury a line from the house so Rosie's retreat could have electricity. He hung a pretty stained glass light fixture featuring apples from the middle of the room and installed several outlets. "Now you can plug in your little boom box or even a portable refrigerator," Grandpa said. "And when you're older, you'll need a study lamp and a place for your laptop computer."

Grandpa found a nice wooden table with spindle legs at a yard sale, and three matching chairs to go with it. He sanded them all until they were smooth, painted them the color of white camellia blossoms, and set the table against one of the windows facing the big house. Grandma June made nice thick cushions that fit in the seats and tied to the back of the chair. The cushions were the color of strawberries, made of the same material as the bright curtains. They matched up nicely with the tweed fabric in the worn sofa and chair that came from her grandparents' own house, because they were getting a new set.

The sofa went against the end of the playhouse on the opposite side from the table, and the chair and its matching ottoman were set beside it, and Grandpa went to the flea market and found an end table and a lamp to go in the corner between them. On the back wall across from the table, Grandpa built a counter top that had cabinets beneath and shelves above so Rosie would have a place to store books or toys that she wanted to keep there. Grandma gave her a picture Bible to keep on the shelf, and a set of Nancy Drew mysteries. The last thing Grandpa did was to install a locking doorknob so Rosie could feel more secure, and he put the key on a keychain attached to a little flashlight.

Rosie thought her playhouse was like a little spot of heaven on earth. She went out to it every day when she came home from school. After supper, it was Rosie's job to clean the table and wash the dishes. Then, while her mother read celebrity magazines and Dan watched TV with a beer in one hand and a remote in the other, Rosie would steal out to her sanctuary and play with her dolls and stuffed animals. She kept them neatly arranged on the shelves Grandpa had built. Rosie liked to sit two or three of them on the table and set out little cups and saucers and have a tea party. Rosie always invited her favorite teddy bear, whose name was Billingsworth, and she alternated the other guests. They drank pretend tea and had witty conversations about what the other stuffed animals had been up to that day.

As Rosie grew older, there was less time for tea parties because she was more likely to spread out books and homework assignments on her table. Her teddy bear and the other shelf-dwellers watched while Rosie added sums and practiced long division. Then, she would go to her big chair and put her feet on the ottoman and do her reading.

Sometimes, on the weekends, Rosie stayed in her playhouse so long that she fell asleep on the couch and didn't wake up until the next morning. Mitzi and Dan didn't seem to mind, but it bothered Rosie a little that they didn't worry about her more.

One weekend, Dan and Mitzi sent Rosie to stay with her grand-parents because they were planning a big party for some of their friends and they didn't want her around. The party turned out to be bigger than they planned, however. Skeeter wasn't invited, but he came anyway and brought some muscular friends who never took off their sunglasses. Dan and Mitzi had run up quite a debt buying meth from Skeeter, and the pusher had run out of patience. When they couldn't pay, he sent his friends to trash the house and look for any money or jewelry or nice things that could be pawned. Two of them went out to Rosie's playhouse and kicked in the door and ransacked everything inside.

While the muscle guys were outside, Mitzi called the police, who showed up too late to catch Skeeter, but in plenty of time to notice evidence of drug use. They searched the main house for any stash that might be hidden, and then went through Rosie's little house. They arrested Mitzi and Dan for possessing drug paraphernalia and on sus-picion that they might be part of Skeeter's network.

Nobody thought to call Rosie, so when Grandpa brought her home late Sunday afternoon at the appointed time, they were startled to find a detective in the yard, balling up the remains of yellow crime scene tape that had once circled the house. Rosie stepped carefully inside to find the house empty of people but full of trash, and through the window she could see that the door to her playhouse was open. Before Grandpa could stop her, she ran across the yard and stood in the doorway of her little house. Muddy footprints scarred the carpet. The cabinet doors hung open, and games and books were scattered across the floor. Rosie's dolls had been thrown this way and that, and some of the stuffed animals had been slit open to see if anything was hidden inside.

Rosie scooped up Billingsworth and tried to push the foam stuff-ing back into his belly, but she couldn't make it stay. With her flattened teddy bear clutched tightly to her chest, Rosie crawled under the table and collapsed in a quivering torrent of tears. When Grandpa caught up, he carefully got down on his knees and crept under the table and crouched beside Rosie. He rubbed her back and hummed an old hymn but didn't say anything at all, because he knew there was nothing to say.

It wasn't long before Rosie's sobs began to lessen, and she slowly formed a firm resolve that Grandpa could feel rising in her back, which was no longer bent and heaving, but now straight and calm. "I've got some cleaning up to do, Grandpa," she said. "I'm going to scrub the badness back out of here and make it a place of goodness again."

And with that, Rosie clambered out from under the table and set about putting things in order. Grandpa Jim used his cell phone to call Grandma, and June soon arrived in her old but still shiny gold Buick. She brought Jim's toolbox and her own sewing kit, so Grandpa could repair the broken lock while she mended the stuffed animals as best she could, leaving only the smallest of scars. Meanwhile, Rosie scrubbed at the muddy carpet with a brush and cleaner she brought from the house. When everything was set as right as it could be, Rosie asked Grandma and Grandpa to stand in a circle with her and hold hands while she said a prayer asking God to make her little house a place where only goodness was at home.

A policeman brought Mitzi and Dan back from the station after they signed a note promising to appear for a court date later in the month, and they were surprised to find Rosie and her grandparents hard at work cleaning up the mess in their house, too. Mitzi felt ashamed and embarrassed. Dan was so mad at Skeeter that he couldn't think of anything else.

And that's how life was for Rosie while she was a child. Like a rose among thorns, she flourished despite adversity, and neighbors wondered how she managed so well. But time passed and Rosie grew, as children do. Years went by, and Rosie began to spend more and more time with her friends, while spending less and less time in her little house or with her grandparents.

As it often happens, some of Rosie's friends were prone to misbehaving. Rosie didn't like it, but she didn't want to lose her friends. As time went by, they teased her and tried persuading her to join them. They told her she needed to loosen up. They promised her more fun than she ever had before. Rosie wanted to have fun, and she wanted to fit in with her friends. She resisted mightily, but eventually she started behaving more like her friends than like the person she wanted to be.

Rosie did have fun, but she noticed that it never lasted for very long, and it usually left her feeling bad. Late one night, after coming home from a party, she stumbled into the house and went to the kitchen in search of something to eat or drink to hide the smell of liquor on her breath. While she stood at the sink eating chocolate ice cream from the carton, Rosie looked out the window and noticed her little house standing in the moonlight, beckoning. A faint, warm glow came from the windows because Rosie always left a nightlight burning beside the sofa.

Rosie put the ice cream back in the freezer and picked up her pocketbook. She walked out to the little house and looked through the windows in the door and put her key in the lock. Rosie stood there blinking against the hot tears that burned her eyes for several minutes, but she couldn't bring herself to turn the key or open the door. On the wall above the nightlight, she could see the little cardboard poster she had painted and hung beside her chair years before. It said "Rosie's Retreat: Where Goodness Is at Home."

Rosie was feeling everything but goodness. She wanted to go inside as she did in more innocent days. She wanted to lie back in the big chair and look out through the skylight and try to count the stars. She wanted to sit warm and secure and talk to God the way she used to, but she felt the weight of darkness pressing on her. Rosie no longer felt like a good person. She sensed that the darkness and chaos she felt inside would violate the blessings she had put on the little house years before. She no longer felt worthy to enter a house where only goodness is at home.

Rosie took the key from the door and dropped it into her pocketbook, where it jangled as it rubbed against her car keys and the little flashlight she still carried. She went back to the house and crawled into bed and cried as she had not cried since the day she had found Billingsworth with his stuffing hanging out.

A raucous ring tone on her cell phone awakened Rosie the next morning. It was Grandma June calling to see if she would join them for church and a big Sunday lunch. "We haven't seen you much lately," Grandma said. "We miss you, dear, and would love to spend some time with you. And, I'm fixing your favorite lasagna!"

Rosie's dry mouth and queasy stomach felt in no shape for lasagna, but her heart longed for the warmth of her grandparents' house, their hugs, and their no-questions-asked kind of love. And so Rosie dragged herself from bed. She showered and dressed and pulled her bright hair back with a clip, then tiptoed past the snoring sounds coming from Mitzi and Dan's room.

Rosie hadn't been too sure about going back to church, but she sat willingly beside Grandpa Jim and smiled at Grandma June, who looked like an angel in her white choir robe with the golden V-necked stole. The choir sang a beautifully harmonized version of "Amazing Grace," and Rosie closed her eyes to let the warm sound of it sweep over her. She was a little surprised, when she opened her eyes, to discover that they were wet.

As the last chord of the hymn died away, Pastor Bill came to the pulpit with a smile that clearly did not come from a can. Rosie had always liked that about him. He always appeared genuine and honest. When he told Rosie that he cared for her and would pray for her, she believed it was true.

Pastor Bill stood at the pulpit and opened his worn Bible with the black leather cover and the gold-edged paper, and he prepared to read from somewhere that appeared to be very near the end.

"Our Scripture for today is a text that was made for people who are facing trials and troubles," said Pastor Bill. "It is a text for people who wonder how long they can go on with life the way it is. It is a text for those of us who are feeling torn on the inside, and who seek the peace of God's eternal promise to replace the chaos of our present reality.

"Hear now these words from the second letter attributed to the Apostle Peter, chapter three, verses eight to fifteen. The writer is nearing the end of his letter. He is writing to people who are dear to him, but who face very trying, very troublesome times, and this is what he says:

But do not ignore this one fact, beloved, that with the Lord one day is like a thousand years, and a thousand years are like one day.

The Lord is not slow about his promise, as some think of slowness, but is patient with you, not wanting any to perish, but all to come to repentance.

But the day of the Lord will come like a thief, and then the heavens will pass away with a loud noise, and the elements will be dissolved with fire, and the earth and everything that is done on it will be disclosed.

Since all these things are to be dissolved in this way, what sort of persons ought you to be in leading lives of holiness and godliness, waiting for and hastening the coming of the day of God, because of which the heavens will be set ablaze and dissolved, and the elements will melt with fire?

But, in accordance with his promise, we wait for new heavens and a new earth, where righteousness is at home.

Therefore, beloved, while you are waiting for these things, strive to be found by him at peace, without spot or blemish; and regard the patience of our Lord as salvation.

Rosie caught her breath: the pastor had almost lost her with the loud noise and the dissolving fire and the melting elements, but then she heard these words that landed on her heart like snow on a cedar: ". . . in accordance with his promise, we wait for new heavens and a new earth, where righteousness is at home."

Rosie knew that more than anything in the world, she wanted to feel once again that righteousness was at home in her heart. She drank in every word as the pastor talked about repentance and forgiveness and God's willing acceptance of all who trust in Jesus' free offer of grace. When the choir stood and sang "Just As I Am, Without One Plea," she wanted to go forward and pray at the altar, but she didn't. Something inside her said "Wait; not here."

As the last notes of the choral benediction hung in the air, Rosie turned to Grandpa and rapidly said she was sorry but she'd had a change of plans and she couldn't come to dinner because there was something else she had to do. She promised she would call them soon. Before Jim could respond, she slipped out the side door and drove home as fast as she safely could.

Rosie sat in the car for a thoughtful moment, then walked around the garage and straight to the little house in the backyard. Trembling, she put the key in the lock, and without hesitating, she opened the door.

June looked troubled when she met Jim outside the choir room and he explained to her how Rosie had rushed out after the service. They drove thoughtfully home and June quietly checked to make sure the oven timer had worked correctly, then took the lasagna out and set it on the counter to cool a bit. She put some garlic toast in the oven and was tossing the salad when the phone rang. Grandpa Jim picked it up.

He listened for a moment as an enormous grin spread beneath his bushy moustache. "It's Rosie," he said. "She wants to know if we can bring the lasagna over, and join her for lunch in her little house. She says there's been a makeover there, and goodness is at home."

A CANNIBAL LECTURE
John 6:51-58

AARGH'S ADVENTURE

A vulture circles lazily in the air above the grassy savannahs of what is now western Turkey, but 40,000 years ago it was called "Ugha." The vulture climbs slowly on heat waves rising from the grassy plain, then dips toward the foothills of the Taurus mountains. The great bird is looking for something to eat, preferably something dead.

High on the side of a rocky crag, the vulture focuses on something that interests her. It is a man. Perhaps you can see him there, too. He is crouching behind a boulder, wearing nothing at all except for a rawhide thong tied around his neck. There is a heavy stick in his hand. A sharp point carefully knapped from dark gray flint is lashed to one end of the stick with another strip of rawhide. Sweat drips from the man's hairy body as he waits, with every muscle tensed and ready for action.

The man's name is Aargh. His mother was called Angha, and his father was Urgh. Just a few moments before the vulture spotted him, the man had stifled an "Aargh!" behind clenched teeth, and with good reason. He had gone out that morning in search of a careless mountain goat, but had found something more careful than he. From the corner of one eye, the hunter had seen a brief flash of tawny fur: a sabertooth was stalking him.

Aargh knew that if the giant cat caught him on the flat land, he would have no chance of survival: his long life of twenty-two years would be over. And so it was that he hunkered down behind the big boulder, where there was a drop in the trail. He was naked now because he had left his loincloth on the trail just above him, to the right of the boulder. Aargh knew that the big tooth would stop to sniff at his scent, and perhaps to taste the leather. He knew that his life depended on that moment of distraction.

From the shadow of the boulder, Aargh listened to the tiny sounds made by the heavy animal's padded feet. With every muscle taut and every hair on his back standing at nervous attention, he waited until the sabertooth glided around the corner and turned briefly to the bait. Like a spring unleashed, Aargh dove at the beast, drove his spear deep into the animal's broad chest, and left it there. He then leapt to the top of the rock as the big cat took off like a shot, then collapsed and writhed in bloody agony. When the animal finally stopped moving, Aargh lifted his face to the sky and cried "*Aargh!*"

Wouldn't you?

Aargh was the first person in his clan ever to have killed a sabertooth. Indeed, he was the first to have survived a sabertooth. The people of his cave were so excited that when they came to help carry the carcass home, they grunted and hooted and danced all the way back to camp.

Aargh used a heavy rock to break the huge fangs from the cat's massive head. He gave one great tooth to his father, who was the old man of the clan. The other he wore around his neck on the rawhide thong, with the animal's largest claws on either side.

That night he sat around the fire with his clan, and he shared with them the tough but tasty flesh of the fierce predator. As he ate, Aargh though to himself, *Aargh aargh aarghaarghaargh aargh, Aargh!*—which in translation means "I eat big tooth. His blood my blood. His strength my strength. I am *Aargh!*"

KIMBA'S REVENGE

Deep in the jungles of eastern Borneo, maybe four hundred years ago, there was a rustle in the night, a scream, and a menacing laugh. A boy named Kimbo, in the midst of his eighth year, peered through the bamboo walls of his open-air hut and saw the dark bodies of large men running through the village. They were stealing women, especially the young ones, and killing any of the half-wakened men who tried to make a defense. The leader of the group stood on the edge of the circle of huts and shook his spear just before the raiding party left. "I Tonga!" he cried. "Remember, and be afraid!"

Kimbo was indeed afraid, and he burned the name Tonga into his memory as he watched the cruel man drag his sister into the brush and out of his young life. In the darkness of his hut, young Kimbo made a promise to himself that one day he would be big and strong. One day he would avenge his sister. One day Tonga would know *his* name, and fear.

It was some five years later when Kimbo met Tonga again. He had just passed the test of manhood by spending a full night alone in the forest at the dark of the moon, and surviving. The elders did not know it and would not have allowed it, but Kimbo had spent the night floating silently down the river to discover where Tonga's people lived before finding his way back in the gray light of dawn.

The chief pronounced his man-name to be Kimba, and he became a big man in the tribe. Kimba proved himself to be an excellent hunter: when he took his bow and his blowgun into the forest, he came back with meat more often than anyone. Kimba shared the meat, but kept his secrets.

Kimba hunted alone, often slipping away from the others so he could venture closer and closer to the village where Tonga lived. Kimba learned where the game trails were, where the men of Tonga's tribe liked to hunt, and where the best places for hiding could be found.

And so it was that Kimba found the perfect spot for ambush, and he was waiting there one misty morning when Tonga went out to hunt. As Tonga crept through a leafy glade while peering into the trees for game, he never imagined that an enemy might be waiting for him in the roots of the big banyan tree beside the deer track. It came as quite a surprise, then, when Tonga felt the bite of Kimba's poisoned dart digging into the flesh of his bare thigh. He gave chase, but the poison quickly took effect. Tonga lived just long enough to see Kimba standing above him with a sharp stone dagger in his hand, and to hear him shout, "Know me and die: I Kimba!"

That night Kimba shared the body of Tonga with the people of his village, for they were indeed headhunters and that was their way of life. Though they all drank from Tonga's blood and shared his flesh, Kimba kept the heart of his enemy for himself, and as he chewed the tough muscle, he said to himself "Tonga life now in me. Tonga power my power. *I Kimba!*"

JESUS' TROUBLESOME TALK
(John 6:51-58)

In the town of Capernaum, a sizable crowd of local citizens, traveling curiosity seekers, and synagogue officials surrounded a curious man named Jesus and tried to make sense of his teaching. The theologians were furious, shouting to one and all that Jesus was teaching a dangerous and tasteless heresy. People of less education were more apt to be confused by it all, and the disciples were among them.

And what was Jesus teaching? Hear it for yourself: "Very truly, I tell you," Jesus was saying, "unless you eat the flesh of the Son of Man and drink his blood, you have no life in you. Those who eat my flesh and drink my blood have eternal life, and I will raise them up on the last day; for my flesh is true food and my blood is true drink. Those who eat my flesh and drink my blood abide in me, and I in them. Just as the living Father sent me, and I live because of the Father, so whoever eats me will live because of me. This is the bread that came down from heaven, not like that which your ancestors ate, and they died. But the one who eats this bread will live forever." (John 6:53-58)

Everything Jesus said in that remarkable speech sounded like an abominable violation of Jewish law. Jews were not allowed to eat any meat that had blood in it, even the blood of sheep or goats. That is one of the reasons for their careful system of offering sacrifices, in which the priest saw that the blood was properly drained and took his portion and declared that the rest was fit for consumption.

The Torah taught that life was a gift of God, and the life of an animal was in the blood. Both blood and life belonged to God alone.

How could Jesus speak in such a graphic and heretical way? Did he expect his followers to be some kind of disgusting cannibals, eating the flesh and drinking the blood of their own master?

No one who heard Jesus teach that day went home comfortable— or hungry, either, for that matter. When we read this story almost 2,000 years later, it still makes us both uneasy and a bit queasy.

You may even feel a little put out with Jesus, just as the religious people of his own day were angry with him. Why did he have to be so controversial? Why couldn't he pick a nicer metaphor? And it *was* a metaphor, wasn't it? Just what *was* Jesus trying to do?

What, indeed?

For one thing, he got our attention, didn't he? That's part of what Jesus was trying to do. In our world, sometimes you will hear somebody make some outrageous claim, and when others look to see if it is true, he will say, "Made you look!" When Jesus made some of his more outrageous statements, you can almost hear him saying, "Made you *think!*"

Jesus makes us *think*. Think, for example, about what has happened in this sixth chapter of John. The chapter opened with Jesus feeding a large multitude of people by the miraculous multiplication of a few fish and barley loaves. On the next day, many of those who had eaten the night before came in search of Jesus again. They were seeking more bread from heaven, and Jesus promised that he would indeed give to them the true bread that comes down from God in heaven (vv. 25-34). Does that bother anybody? Of course not.

With verses 35-51, Jesus moved from a meal to a metaphor, pushing his hearers a bit deeper in their understanding of him. Jesus had promised to provide the bread that gives life to his followers. Then he said, "*I'm* the bread!"

What?

"I am the bread of life." If you are looking for life, Jesus said, you've come to the right place. "I'm the bread of life."

Does that bother us? No. We don't mind talking about Jesus as the bread of life, so long as it remains in the abstract. In fact, we've grown quite accustomed to that image. We like it.

But then in verses 52-58, Jesus puts two and two together and pushes the metaphor to its natural conclusion. If Jesus *gives* the bread of life, and Jesus *is* the bread of life, then one who wants the bread of life must seek Jesus. Now, bread does us no good until we eat it and it becomes a part of us. Thus, coming to Jesus does no good unless we find a way to bring Jesus into our lives, and the natural metaphor Jesus used was *eating*. Still has an uncomfortable feel, doesn't it?

I think Jesus stuck with this troublesome metaphor because he wanted his hearers to understand that God did not just come to humankind through some intangible essence, but through the physical reality of Jesus himself. God is not just to be thought of as an eternal principle, but an active participant in our lives. And it is only through participating in *his* life that we can find the abundant and eternal life the Bible says he came to give. We participate through trusting Jesus and accepting his grace.

Our Remarkable Opportunity

Understanding this incredible, troubling text helps us to appreciate why Jesus chose to have his disciples remember him through the observance we now call "the Lord's Supper" or "Holy Communion." *What did Jesus say as he distributed bread and wine to his friends?* "This is my body that is broken for you. Take, and eat. This is my blood that is shed for you. Drink it in remembrance of me" (Luke 22:19).

With the institution of the Lord's Supper, Jesus offers us an interpretive key to his earlier discussion that sounded so much like cannibalism. It should be obvious that Jesus never intended for his disciples to take a bite out of his arm. But he was deadly serious about their need to receive his living reality into their lives.

The material substances of bread and wine remind us of the present reality of Jesus Christ. It is not necessary for us to get involved in endless theological debates about transubstantiation or consubstantiation, trying to imagine if the bread and wine truly become the body and blood of Christ, and if so, when. The issue is not about what we are eating, but our willingness to receive it.

The tangible symbols of Communion, bread that is broken and grapes that are crushed, are precious gifts of God. They bring to us in a present way the incarnate reality of Jesus Christ, who truly came to live among us, who taught us the way of life, who was broken for our sins and rose again to God's glory.

They bring us into the presence of Jesus, who said, "I am the living bread that came down from heaven. Whoever eats of this bread will live forever; and the bread that I will give for the life of the world is my flesh" (v. 51).

Who said, "Unless you eat the flesh of the Son of Man and drink his blood, you have no life in you" (v. 53).

Who said, "Those who eat my flesh and drink my blood have eternal life, and I will raise them up on the last day; for my flesh is true food and my blood is true drink" (v. 55).

Who said, "Those who eat my flesh and drink my blood abide in me, and I in them" (v. 56).

Who said, "Just as the living Father sent me, and I live because of the Father, so whoever eats me will live because of me" (v. 57).

Who said, "This is the bread that came down from heaven, not like that which your ancestors ate, and they died. But the one who eats this bread will live forever" (v. 58).

Who said, "This is my body, which is given for you" (Luke 22:19a).

Who said, "This cup that is poured out for you is the new covenant in my blood" (Luke 22:20).

Who said, "Do this in remembrance of me" (Luke 22:19b).

Let's *do!*

GREEN MOUNTAIN ROCKS
Luke 10:29-37

DREAMING DREAMS

Off in the western stretches of the mountainous Kingdom of Cleft, at the end of the trail in a place that few visitors ever reached, a craggy peak raised its angled crest into the deep blue sky. The place was called Green Mountain, not just because of the mighty trees upon its lower slopes, but on account of the rocky outcrops that sparkled clear and green when the sun broke through the clouds.

The color came from thick veins of obsidian that were formed as volcanic magma that had surfaced thousands of years before. Trace elements in the obsidian's silica base gave rise to the emerald tint in the shining stone.

At the foot of Green Mountain there was a deep divide, a steep and narrow chasm cracked open by the same Vulcan forces that had pushed up the mountain behind. Locals called it the Black Crack, and though many had tried, no one had made a rope long enough to plumb its depths. Sometimes, sulfurous fumes would drift up from below.

The canyon was hardly more than fifty feet wide, but it may as well have been a mile, for the sides were so sheer and the defile so deep that no one could cross it. The Black Crack ran for miles and miles both north and south from the mountain's foothills, and there were other dangers in both directions, so few people ever traveled to the glittering mountain.

Among those who never set foot on the Green Mountain was an entire village of people who lived in its shadow. They dwelt just opposite the mountain and its deep divide, in a small valley whose fields were fertile and well watered and beautifully tended. A cheerful stream that made its way through the valley exchanged its chatter for a roar when it tumbled into the Black Crack, and the villagers could only guess at how far the water fell or where it went on its subterranean journey.

The valley was so small that its residents did not wish to waste a single acre, so they built their homes right along the rocky side of the deep gorge, where the soil was shallow and the crops did not grow. The name of the town was Rakestraw, and all of its people were farmers, dark of skin from a life so close to the sun in their highland home.

To protect themselves, they wore pointed straw hats so distinctive that throughout the kingdom they were known as Rakestraw bonnets.

Now, to say that the people of Rakestraw were isolated is not to say that they had no neighbors, because just across the Black Crack, nestled against the side of the mountain, there was a tiny settlement of homes skillfully built from smooth granite blocks that were artfully inlaid with the Green Mountain stone. The village was so small that the people of Rakestraw called it "Thimble." They did not know what the Green Mountain people called their village, because those people spoke a language unknown to anyone else in the Kingdom of Cleft. Wind-borne words sometimes traveled across the ravine, but to the people of Rakestraw, they were all gibberish.

In many ways, the residents of Thimble were a mystery to the people of Rakestraw, but they could tell the Thimbletonians were an industrious people. They tended sheep and raised vegetables in steep hillside plots. They wore striking pants and capes and floppy hats made of wool dyed purple and orange and green. And, sitting beneath the shade of the beeches and elms that surrounded Green Mountain, they worked with the emerald-colored stone. They hammered and chiseled and shaped and polished the stone, making beautiful dishes and ornamental figures and delicate jewelry.

So it was that the two villages existed within a few hundred feet of each other, but the people lived as complete strangers. And, because the people of Rakestraw and Thimble did not know each other, it was a given that they disliked each other. Each village imagined that the other had a richer or better location, for the people of Rakestraw coveted the green stone of Thimble and the people of Thimble envied the green fields of Rakestraw. Day by day, the villagers lived in a state of mutual jealousy and suspicion: for all that they saw each other, there was no real contact between the villages, no conversation at all. Most people never considered the possibility of communicating with their neighbors, nor could they imagine why anyone would want to. That is just the way things were.

But there was a boy in the town of Thimble who was not satisfied with the way things were. His given name was Guldorf, but most people called him "Slam," which was the Thimbletonian word for "hammer."

As the boy grew tall and broad-shouldered, he worked hard and paid attention, and in time, Slam became the best stonecutter and builder in the village. He seemed to have been born with a mallet in one hand and a chisel in the other.

Slam wanted more than the prestige of mastering his craft, however. He had dreams, big dreams. Slam's thinking went beyond hammers and chisels and building more stone houses. He dreamed of what lay beyond the Black Crack.

About the time Slam reached his fortieth birthday, it happened that old man Farley surrendered to senility after many years of serving as village chief. The elders reverently committed Farley's body to the depths of the Black Crack, and then held a solemn council to choose a new leader. In short order, they appointed Slam to take over as chief, and the respected craftsman applied himself with great energy to the new role. As time went by, he continued to win the confidence of all the people in Thimble.

Slam paid close attention to the mood of his fellow villagers, and he kept a wary eye on the people beyond the crack, and always he was thoughtful. One evening in the fall of the year, after the crops had been laboriously brought in from their steep mountain plots, Slam called a village meeting around a roaring bonfire. There, amid the flickering glow and dancing shadows, he set forth an idea he had been working on since he was a boy.

It should be said that the plan did not go over well on first hearing. In fact, it was greeted with much shaking of heads and wagging of tongues and some brandishing of fists. In time, however, Slam convinced his neighbors that the time had come to stop sitting back and waiting. It was time to rise up and do something about those strange people across the canyon.

So it happened that the residents of Rakestraw woke up one morning to find that the Thimbletonians had been hard at work since before sunup. Men and women were going back and forth up and down the mountain, leading their little burros, bringing loads of the biggest rocks their sturdy beasts could carry. Others were dragging the trunks of newly felled trees to the edge of the valley, and great coils of heavy rope, and sharpened spikes. Already, there was a considerable pile of stones and wood, and it was growing.

When word came to the mayor, he called an emergency meeting of his village council. "What can they be doing?" he asked. "And how should we respond?"

There was only one answer, of course. A bony farmer named Hiram Ham stood up and stated the obvious: "Well mayor, it looks like they're collectin' rocks for ammunition. Soon they'll build catapults from them wooden beams and ropes they're piling up over there, and then they'll attack us!"

Stringer Plotz joined in. "I'll bet they's got an army that's already marched around the Black Crack and hid in our fields. Once they've pounded us with rocks from them catapults they's gettin' ready to build, their soldiers will rush in and take over our town and steal our crops. Boys, we gotta defend ourselves!"

And before the mayor could even call for a vote, the councilmen rushed out and commandeered every person they could find. They ranged over the farmlands and started hauling in the fieldstones they had collected and built into fences when they had cleared their land years before. Soon, they had a mound of rocks on their side of the valley to match the stones piling up across the way. They pulled down an old barn and dragged its large beams to the brink of the valley so they could build their own catapults and fight fire with fire and stone with stone.

By the time the people of Rakestraw had gathered their stores, however, they came to realize that the Thimbletonians were not building catapults after all. They were digging deep foundations and making strong stanchions firm within them. They were pounding spikes and lashing beams together in long, straight lines. They were setting the beams hard against the stone to make strong scaffolding that was already reaching out over the chasm.

They were building a bridge.

In their growing awareness of what was taking place, the leaders of Rakestraw were caught quite off guard. They weren't sure what to make of this. Did those people think they could just build a bridge in peace and then waltz across it to conquer their town? They could not stand by and let such a thing happen.

But what they saw and what they thought did not add up. If the people of Thimble were interested in aggression, surely they would have had weapons at the ready—but the men on the growing bridge were armed only with smiles. A large man was encouraging them, waving a big hammer like a conductor's baton, grinning like a happy child and occasionally waving at the curious people who stood across the canyon.

Finally, the mayor of Rakestraw realized what was happening. The people of Thimble were industriously working on a job they could not possibly finish alone. They were trusting that their neighbors would see the wisdom of their plan and start working from their side of the crack and meet them in the middle.

The mayor summoned the most skilled builders in Rakestraw to calculate how they could best set to work. He called on his people to fetch their shovels, to dig their own foundations, to sink deep supports into their side of the rocky divide, and to fasten the longest and strongest beams together.

It was nearly nightfall when Mayor Thornburg and Chief Slam walked solemnly to the middle of the bridge and exchanged hats. They could not understand each other's language, but they both understood that a new day was coming. Their isolation was ending. Trust would grow like wheat in the fields around Rakestraw. Friendships would emerge like the finest green jewelry in Thimble.

And all because of a bridge whose first foundation was built in the heart of a boy named Slam.

BUILDING BRIDGES

This little story doesn't sound much like a Bible story, and it isn't, but the theme of the story is very much a biblical theme.

The story about the man we call "The Good Samaritan" (Luke 10:29-37) is one of the best-known and most-loved stories in the Bible—and one of the most ignored. It is the story Jesus told in response to the question, "Who is my neighbor?" It is the story of a simple man who built bridges of friendship and caring when other men would not. It is a story about reaching across the deep cultural divide that separated Jews from Samaritans and bridging the gap of distrust with compassion.

That's an attractive thought, isn't it? The concept of bridge building is appealing to us. But how many of us have shovels or hammers in our hands?

It takes little effort to think of people in our communities, people as close in proximity as Rakestraw and Thimble, who may feel alienated by deep divides that may be racial or cultural or economic. Others may be isolated by age or health or physical handicaps.

Can we think of specific, practical ways in which we can build bridges of friendship to those persons, even if they have not asked us to come to them?

The question is not whether we have hammers. The question is what we plan to do with them.

HOW RAE GOT THE VOODOO

1 Samuel 28:3-25

HOW RAE GOT THE VOODOO

Rae was nine years old when her Aunt Van empowered her with the "gift" of removing warts, but she didn't think much of it at the time. She just liked hanging out with her aunt, a cranky old maid whose real name was "Savannah." Rae, whose given name was Ramona, knew that Aunt Van liked her almost as much as she liked dipping Navy brand "Sweet Scotch" snuff and drinking Four Roses Kentucky Straight Bourbon Whiskey.

Van was a certified spinster who never married because she couldn't get the man she wanted and wouldn't have the men she could get. More than once, so say the stories, men who drove into her yard with courtship on their minds rode away with bullet holes in their buggy tops.

Van's home was a weathered old house that had never been painted. There was a worn hole through the wall in the west gable that she claimed was once used for shooting at Indians. There was another hole in a corner of the floor behind her food-encrusted kerosene stove, and she used it when throwing out the dishwater or bathwater on those occasions when she reckoned some measure of cleanliness was in order. The water came from a good well in the front yard, where she used a bucket attached to a windlass and chain to draw her daily supply. The old house is gone now, but the well remains as a rustic decoration outside the fine home and antique car garage that Little Roy Lewis built after he bought the property.

While the sagging house still stood, however, whenever young Rae crossed the road and strutted in, Aunt Van was likely to wring the neck of a chicken and fry it up in the same cast iron skillet she used to threaten gentlemen callers. She always gave Rae a leg with the thigh still attached, because she thought that was the most flavorful piece.

Truth be told, Rae was about the only relative that Van cared for. She didn't get along with her brothers Bent or Ode or even sweet Aunt Dora and Uncle Babe. After her health started breaking down, the younger kinfolk put her in a nursing home where she raised such a ruckus that the nurses tied her to the bed before Rae persuaded them to keep her dosed with whiskey. Despite her lack of teeth, Rae says, Van got her a boyfriend there and was the happiest she'd ever been until the day she fell.

She fell, and the fall broke one of her hips, and Van died shortly after, leaving a will that bequeathed everything she owned to a young fellow who had kept her stocked with government (tax paid) liquor to supplement the moonshine and wine she made for herself.

She left him everything, that is, except the gift of removing warts, which she had already given to Rae.

Being so young and all, Rae had given little thought to the gift Aunt Van had passed down in carefully whispered instructions that she was sworn to keep secret on pain of death or something worse. Sometime later, though, Rae remembered the gift as she walked out of Nell Underwood's store and nearly stumbled over an old dog whose name was Deuce. Rae noticed that the dog had a big wart on his nose. Suddenly inspired, she leaned down and whispered, "Deuce, would you like me to take that wart off?"

Gingerly, Rae touched the warty growth, and blew on it gently, and when she got home she worked Aunt Van's magic spell in a secret place. The next time she went to the store, Deuce's ugly wart was gone.

Laying eyes on that wartless dog nose was a defining moment for Rae, and from that day on she was never quite the same. She cherished her gift, and nurtured it, and smiled in knowing that she harbored a secret power. Still in her teens, she legally changed her given name from "Ramona" to "Rae."

Rae knew she was special.

Rae lived with her mother, Thelma Willis, in a ramshackle cabin they shared with a man named Cliff Mattox, who was not Rae's father. Thelma liked to paint in her spare time, copying calendar pictures onto canvases she would save up to buy. Cliff was known to be part Cherokee, and he was the only man in the county who could creep down to the riverbank and catch a snapping turtle by the tail without the turtle knowing he was coming.

Cliff liked to eat sliced onion sandwiches with mayonnaise, and he would drink anything that held the promise of alcohol. That's why his buddies Aaron and Pete couldn't entirely trust him. They used to make moonshine and put it in gallon jugs and hide what they didn't sell in stump holes out in the Spring Woods behind Van's house. If they didn't keep a close eye, Cliff would sniff out the jugs and drink their stash.

That wouldn't have been so bad, except that Cliff was mean when he got drunk, and Thelma paid for his meanness. They had finally gotten married, and Thelma didn't want to leave him, but sometimes it got bad and she had little choice but to hide out with one of her sisters, Viola or Coonie. They would look after her and put mustard plasters on Thelma's black eyes and sore ribs until she looked presentable again. Then Thelma would go back home.

Rae left as soon as she was old enough, and did not go back.

She married William "Rabbit" Stribling and worked hard and raised three girls and a boy on a 110-acre farm they bought from Mrs. Lula Dorn's estate. Locals knew the farm as "the Brickyard Place" because the bricks for the oldest buildings in town had been dug from its red clay hills, then formed and fired on site. They say that Weems Pennington, the only doctor in the county back then, loaned them the money to buy it. He's dead now, so you can't ask him, but it's the kind of thing he would do.

In time, Rae developed her own reputation as a doctor of sorts, though she has never made any money from it. Rae follows a strict code of ethics common to those who have the gift of wart removal, and the first rule is that she can't take any payment for services rendered. Nor can she remove a wart from anybody who is blood kin. She can never reveal the secret rituals that seal the deal after the public treatment is over. And she can pass on the gift to just one person. She gave it to one of her daughters some time ago, but worries already that she gave it to the wrong one.

You might be wondering just how Rae does what she does. When presented with a wart, Rae examines it closely and rubs it gently while looking directly into her patient's eyes. She requires the person to divulge his or her age, and then offers assurance that the wart will soon be gone. Before they leave, she instructs patients not to look at the wart until it falls off.

"If you keep looking at it, the spell won't work," she tells them. Most of the time, if people follow the rules, the wart will be gone in eight or nine days, she says. The power is tricky, though. It's stronger when she does it at home: only rarely can she remove a wart in town. Sometimes it requires two treatments before the wart is gone, and sometimes they grow back. That's just the way it is with warts.

A local doctor sends people out to see Rae, especially children who get a lot of warts on their hands. He doesn't want to burn off too many warts in one place, particularly when they're near fingernails. One lady brought a van-load of warty kids out for treatment, Rae says, and later reported that all of them got relief except for one little boy, who must have looked at his hands too much.

Eventually, Rae asked the doctor not to send so many people, complaining that they all wanted to stay too long.

It's not surprising that people enjoy visiting the Brickyard Place, because Rae and Rabbit have collected a menagerie of animals ranging from a wild boar and a small herd of goats to loud peacocks and a big flock of white homing pigeons. Some years back, a movie company filming over in South Carolina called to see if she had any black pigeons for a scene they were shooting. Rae dipped a bunch of her white pigeons in black dye and sold the lot. I don't know if they flew home after the scene was shot.

Rae's house is at the end of a narrow dirt drive that winds for nearly half a mile from the state road. She has erected a totem pole and set up fake tombstones here and there, mostly beneath a skeleton that dangles from an overhanging pine tree. The driveway passes by another tree infested with rubber snakes, and then winds through a wrought iron gate that features a golden angel flying above the head of a black goat. Rae says the goat head symbolizes the devil.

The old farmhouse has a neon beer sign in each of the dormer windows, and she lights them up every night. Inside, rambling additions to what started as a small house contain an eclectic collection of treasures harvested at yard sales and estate auctions. Scores of decorative porcelain plates mix with African masks in the front room, and more than 100 wall clocks scattered through the house keep her broke from buying batteries. A painting of a nude woman hangs over the bed in the room behind her voodoo chamber.

Yes, her voodoo chamber: you'd want to know about that. After word got out that Rae could remove warts, superstitious folk figured that she must have other powers, too. Women in unhappy marriages would occasionally sneak out to the farm and ask Rae to make their husbands disappear like an ugly wart. Rae concocted a ritual in which she would light a black candle, give the client a voodoo doll wrapped in gold cloth to hold, and tell her to sit in the voodoo room while rubbing the doll and thinking about what she wanted to happen. Sometimes, it did.

Rae found her newfound reputation invigorating, and she started playing it to the hilt. When one acquaintance asked her to put a hex on her sorry son-in-law, Rae collected some dirt from a graveyard and told the woman to sprinkle it on his apartment's doorstep by moonlight. It didn't work, but Rae insists it was because the woman got confused in the dark and dusted the wrong door.

To reinforce her voodoo reputation, Rae started taking credit for the untimely deaths of anyone she didn't like, including a former policeman who had given her daughter a speeding ticket. Local folk came to fear her hexes so much that she stopped bothering to lock her house.

As Rae's reputation grew, people started coming from all over. She swears that a limousine bearing a millionaire pulled up one night, and as Rae tells it, "an old man riz up out the back seat and said he wanted to buy a chicken." While everyone else went looking for which tree the chickens had picked for a roost, the man stayed behind and confessed that what he really wanted was for Rae to work some voodoo on his wife because she was running around on him.

Rae was not pleased.

Some time later, the man took a fall and broke his leg, his wife left him, and "Everybody got money out of him except me," Rae says. That's okay, though. She took credit for his bad luck because he didn't tell her the truth from the beginning, and it just added to her witchy reputation.

Another old man's daughter-in-law brought him out to Rae's house one day because he claimed he had seen the signs and knew she had voodoo powers. He told her he was in terrible shape, but wanted to get better. Rae picked up a rock from the dirt road and blew on it. She told him to put it in his pocket and rub it every day and think that he was going to get well. She says that he did.

Rae doesn't claim to have all magical powers, though. One day a poor man walked into her yard and said, "I's looking for the fortune teller."

She replied, "If I could tell fortunes, don't you think I would have won the lottery by now?"

He didn't stay long.

Rae hasn't won the lottery, and her 75 years are finally beginning to show, despite her best efforts. Rae's voodoo powers don't work on wrinkles, so at the age of 61, she sold part of the farm to finance a $4,500 facelift. "It's that cotton patch that put the wrinkles on me, and it's going to take them out," she said. She likened her facelift to a new coat of paint on her 1966 Mustang, which has been repainted three times. "I've still got the same motor, I just needed a new coat of paint."

These days, Rae drives a new red Mustang with seven white horses painted on each side. She has had both knees replaced, and several other surgeries on her knees and feet. The foot doctor became so enamored with his patient that he came out to visit her at home and ate all the chicken livers that Rae could fry, straight from the pan.

Rae can't dance and charm the men down at the American Legion every weekend the way she used to, but she still likes to dress well and look good, even if most of the compliments come from men who are stone drunk.

She doesn't go to church much, partly for fear that having a voodoo woman around might make the preacher nervous, but she has her funeral all planned out. One of the two preachers, she says, will be a local pastor who is also an elementary school teacher, the county coroner, and a part-time funeral director. The other preacher on the slate is a man she taught in Vacation Bible School when he was just a boy. Rae doesn't anticipate that the funeral will do her much good, though. She believes in heaven, she says, but fully expects "to be handing out the ice water in hell."

How the Witch of Endor Got Her Ghost

Speaking of death, somewhere around 3,000 years ago, another girl received a special gift, one that led her to believe she could communicate with the dead. This girl lived in the tiny village of Endor, on the north side of the Valley of Jezreel, in a time when the people of Israel were trying a new thing: they had anointed a tall Benjaminite named Saul to rule over them as king.

As Saul grew in power and tried to figure out what it meant to be king, the girl grew in her own place in life as a ghostwife, a necromancer, a medium. Word got around that she could work secretive spells over a ritual pit in the ground and bring up the dead from Sheol.

It was commonly believed in those days that all people went to Sheol when they died, living underground in a shadowy existence that was neither good nor bad. It was also believed that people who had the gift of necromancy could call them up through a sacred fissure in the earth and question them for the benefit of the living.

So it was that, as both of them grew old, a broken-down King Saul came to visit the witchy woman of Endor. Saul had officially banned all spiritists or mediums from the land, but the woman had not left. She just went underground, as it were, kept a low profile and hoped for the best. Nobody turned her in because they never knew when they might need her services. Truth be known, they were a little bit afraid of her, too.

It was a bad time, and Saul was at war, facing a dangerous battle against an overwhelming army of Philistines. Deeply worried, the aging monarch disguised himself in a ratty wig and a decidedly unkingly robe. With two bodyguards, he crept through enemy lines in the dead of night and came to the ghostwife's house, where Saul pleaded with her to call up the prophet Samuel from the dead.

Samuel had not been pleased with Saul when he was alive, and was equally unhappy to be disturbed in death, according to the story in 1 Samuel 28. The only comfort his scowling spirit gave was to tell Saul that he'd be joining him in Sheol the next day. Then, we presume, he could pester Samuel to his heart's content.

Saul was stricken by the news. Deeply distressed, lacking sleep, and famished from a day of fasting, the king collapsed on the floor, presenting the ghostwife with a new problem. She had already seen through Saul's disguise, of course, and had not been happy about it, but he had sworn no harm would come to her. When Saul fell in a heap in the middle of her living room, the old woman responded in a much kinder way than one might expect from a witch. She killed a fatted calf and prepared a meal of bread and meat. She insisted that Saul eat something, even when he resisted. She talked to him like a mama would and told him he would need his strength.

So it was that Saul found no solace from the spirit of Samuel past, but he was comforted by the spiritist woman of the present. He took her words to heart, and ate, and grew strong enough to travel back to the battlefront where he fought bravely and he did die, but it was an honorable death.

How Believers Get the Spirit

As we ponder these stories, a question comes to mind.

What is your gift, and what are you doing with it?

Rae believes she has the gift of wart removal, and she has developed it into a reputation as a full-fledged voodoo woman. Christian believers might find little to praise in her practice of magic-with-a-wink, though she tries to help people in her own way. She makes them feel special and deserving of attention. When she looks into a young boy's eyes and gently rubs his wart and tells him it will get better, that might be the most personal attention he's had in a while. When listening to a woman who wants to make her husband disappear, Rae devotes her full focus to the sad tale, and makes her visitor feel important.

There's something to be said for that.

The so-called "witch of Endor" believed she had the gift of necromancy. We have no way of knowing if she considered it a privilege or a burden, but she did what she believed she was destined to do. Her business was not just with the dead, but with the living. She blessed Saul with motherly kindness on a night when the old king was lost and alone and desperately in need of compassion.

There's something to be said for that, too.

The Bible says plainly that God has spiritual gifts in store for those who will accept them, gifts that are wholly positive, nothing questionable about them. God's giving begins with the offer of salvation: "The wages of sin is death, but the free gift of God is eternal life through Jesus Christ our Lord," Paul said (Rom 3:23).

But that's not all. Paul also spoke, in places like Romans 12 and Ephesians 4, of gifts like preaching and teaching those who need to learn of Christ, ministering to and encouraging those who are downtrodden, practicing hospitality and kindness to those who need the tenderness of someone who cares.

There's something to be said for those gifts, too.

What's being said about you?

> *Author's note:* Unlike the fictional stories that begin other chapters in this collection, Rae's story is true, and told with her permission. Rae Stribling is my second cousin, my grandmother Viola's niece. Lula Dorn was my great-grandmother, who remarried after the death of William Mell Cartledge, my great-grandfather. My father spent the worst years of the Depression helping his mother scratch out a living at the same Brickyard Place, a few miles outside of Lincolnton, Georgia, where Rae now practices her art, raises guineas, and makes a near-magical pound cake.

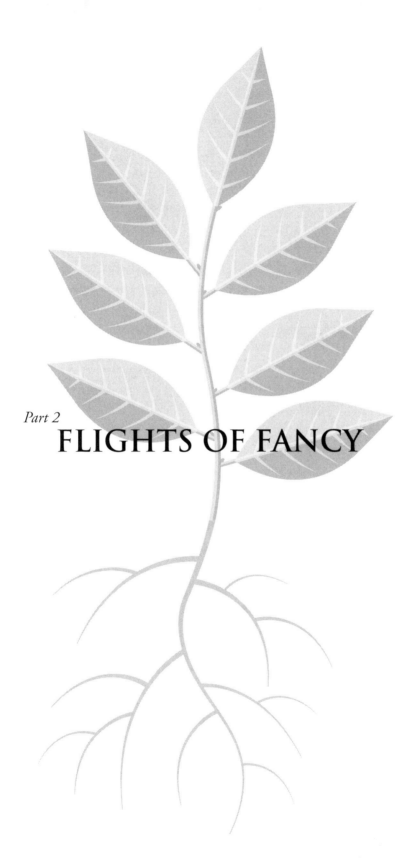

Part 2
FLIGHTS OF FANCY

THE GLIMMERSTONE

Luke 12:16-21

A Prince, a King, and a Fool

The elves were restless, because the Glimmerstone was weeping. There it sat, in its customary place, on the unadorned golden pedestal beside the king's throne in the great hall of the High Mountain Elves.

There it sat, and there it wept. Clear fluid oozed from the sacred stone in syrupy globs that hardened as they fell to the floor, tinkling when they landed in a growing pile of crystal tears that no one dared to touch.

For forty years people had come to admire the stone by the throne, but until now, no one had seen it weep. Even the dullest of the servants could see that the glittering tears were an omen, and they were afraid.

Perhaps you are not familiar with the Glimmerstone? Listen on, then, for it is a tale worth the telling—and the hearing.

The story begins when the king was fully grown, but yet a prince, for his father still lived. The prince's name was Fellyn, and he was tall and fair like his two older brothers, as like unto a mountain elf as any picture you might see in a book. If one could point to any fault in his appearance, it might be that the point on his ears was a bit less pronounced than expected in royalty. Perhaps it was that small touch of the common that fueled the extra zeal with which he pursued whatever agenda lay before him.

It was the custom among the High Mountain Elves that a royal son or daughter would follow their father to the throne, but neither gender nor priority of birth was a consideration, for the elves were more concerned with seeing evidence of wisdom, courage, skill, and other qualities that one might want in a ruler. The kingdom was not quite a democracy as we would know it, for the candidates were generally limited to the king's children. The royal siblings, however, campaigned in their own way for the people's favor, for they knew that the elf who ultimately claimed the throne would be the one acclaimed by the populace as most valiant and most capable of ruling for the good of all.

So it was that Prince Fellyn departed his father's modest castle shortly after completing such education as the royal tutors could offer, and he traveled throughout the kingdom on a quest to do great deeds, display his quality, and strengthen his résumé. In the dusty and isolated hamlet of Redrock, for example, he drew upon knowledge gained from his teachers to show the residents how they could cut cisterns into the stone and apply plaster to the walls, thus preserving the rare rainwater. In this way he helped to make their lives easier and their families healthier.

In the treetop community of Bracken Falls, Fellyn found people who were plagued by poaching from bands of roving chimpanzees that had become increasingly bold. Fellyn used his royal prerogative to order strong ropes from the king's stores and then helped village leaders design a system of sturdy nets to protect the tree-dwellers' food supply from the simian invaders.

For more than half a year, Fellyn settled in one of the kingdom's larger towns, where he showed uncommon wisdom in mediating a longstanding dispute between the civic leaders who wanted to expand the town's borders and the surrounding farmers who did not wish to give up their land.

Fellyn's achievements were impressive, but they were more administrative than heroic, and failed to catch the imagination of the people. He was solid, but not as spectacular as his brother Fenwald, who had slain a rampaging ogre, or his sister Mellon, who had charmed the river trolls into a peace treaty.

So it was that Fellyn continued his wandering pursuit of the glory that had eluded him, and his path ultimately led him to the high village of Aerye, perched among the bare rocks of a soaring mountain crest. Aerye was a mining community where hard-skinned elves coaxed small gemstones from the earth and used them for trade with other towns to obtain their food and clothing.

When Prince Fellyn reached the village, he found a sorrowful and downcast people but little else, for the great dragon Sargon had appeared from the mists of history to afflict their village. Sargon did not hoard gold and silver, like other self-respecting dragons. Only gemstones caught the fell creature's eye, and when he found them, he ate them.

The crafty dragon had learned that salting his internal furnace with gemstones could amplify his natural flame in fortuitous ways. A craw full of emeralds gave Sargon's fiery breath a fearsome greenish hue that sent his enemies into panic. Rubies induced hot red flames that could melt swords of steel, while sapphires burned a brittle blue so bright that with the slightest breath he could hunt at night. But it was diamonds that Sargon coveted most, for with no more than a tiny taste of those rare jewels, he could project a white-hot blaze that could explode the stone of any castle wall. And so Sargon searched for a lasting source of diamonds, thinking they would make him invincible.

By the time Fellyn arrived, the dragon had reduced every building in Aerye to cinders while seeking precious gems to feed his flame. The elves had sought refuge in caves too small for the dragon to enter, but more than one had been roasted by Sargon's angry exhalations.

As the hardened miners wept while telling their story, Fellyn saw immediately that his greatest opportunity lay before him—and his greatest peril. That he must take courage and stand against the marauding dragon was a given. Whether triumph or doom lay beyond, he could not say.

The elves of Aerye knew where the dragon could be found, but neither prodding nor gold could tempt any one of them to guide Fellyn there. "Go yonder," the village chief told him, pointing southward with a thin, worn finger. "You will find him beneath the Head of the Hawk. He ate the last of our ponies just yesterday and could hardly fly away: he'll be sleeping on it for another day yet."

Above the fog-shrouded hills before him, Fellyn's keen eyes could just make out a bare granite outcrop that jutted from a shoulder of the tallest peak. A dark cleft gave the impression of a deep-set eye, and enough soil had eroded from beneath a triangular overhang to shape a wicked beak. Beneath the beak, above the clouds, Fellyn could make out the telltale wisp of smoke that pointed to the dragon's lair.

In hopes of inspiring courage among the villagers, Fellyn defied the dragon by sleeping beneath the stars, then set out at dawn with grim determination, certain that the day's events would bring him lasting fame. The only unknown was whether he would be alive to enjoy it.

In the golden hour before sunset, with a long and winding uphill trek behind him, Fellyn crouched briefly beneath a carnelian sky and peered through the last laurel thicket separating him from the cleft where Sargon slept. He could smell the dragon stench already, and the stone beneath his feet vibrated with the monster's ragged and uneven breath. Fellyn wondered if all dragons breathed that way—and whether they slept lightly.

With the silent tread of a well-trained warrior, the steely-eyed prince crept through stunted hemlocks to climb the last few yards remaining. He did not pause or reconsider or debate what he had to do. He did not pray or test his bow or even take a deep breath. When he reached the edge of cover, Fellyn sprang resolutely into the shadow of the overhang, sword drawn, ready to challenge the murderous beast.

The dragon, however, did not rise to meet him. In fact, the great serpent appeared to be comatose: its color had faded to a dingy, mottled gray. Its breath, though foul, was faint and barely warm. The orange fire was gone from Sargon's wicked eyes. The orbs were open, but covered with a cloudy skim. Whether they even acknowledged the prince's presence, he could not tell.

Now, Fellyn was intelligent enough to know a fortuitous chance when he saw it. He loosened his long spear and raised it. From far enough away to feel safe, yet close enough to be certain of his aim,

Fellyn hurled the bitter shaft so that it sank deep into the dragon's misty eye and penetrated its muddled brain before disintegrating in a flash of light.

The monster died so quickly that it hardly moved at all. Its dreadful tail did not thrash, its mighty wings did not beat against the granite overhang, its cruel teeth did not reach out for the tall elf who had punctuated his life with a sharp, lethal period. In a matter of moments, Sargon lay unmoving beside a trickling, steaming pool of blood as thick and black as the gathering night.

With a good supply of wood nearby, the ambitious prince built a roaring bonfire on the wide rock shelf beneath the Head of the Hawk. Far below, the inhabitants of Aerye saw the flames and mourned for the prince, for they were certain that Sargon was slowly roasting the royal son for his evening's entertainment.

What the villagers could not see was how quickly Fellyn worked in the flickering light to carve the monster into so many pieces that no dragon magic could bring him to life again. It was in the process of cutting off the frightful head, as Fellyn hacked at the hard scales and gave thanks for his keen elvish blade, that he learned the truth of Sargon's demise. Wedged firmly in the dragon's throat was a large clear stone that glimmered in the firelight. Sargon must have seen it on some rocky outcrop and thought he had found the mother of all diamonds, but his eyes were bigger than his throat. The glittering stone had choked him near enough to death that the prince could easily finish the job.

Fellyn pulled the stone free and wiped it clean. It was not an especially shapely stone, and certainly no diamond, but a large piece of clear quartz crystal that had probably oozed from the side of some ancient volcano. Embedded within the crystal were a thousand tiny flecks of shining mica that caused the stone to glimmer warmly in the firelight. The dragon's flame had melted the sharp edges from the stone, leaving it rounded and smooth.

His heart still high on triumph, the young prince caught upon the idea of making the bright stone his personal talisman of power. He christened it the Glimmerstone, and imagined that when he sat upon the throne, he would have the royal artisans mount it beside the dais.

With a perpetual flame burning nearby, he thought, the stone's radiant glow would fill the great hall of the High Mountain Elves and inspire all who came to call.

Of course, Fellyn could never admit that he had killed a dead dragon. Instead, when the time came for recounting his deeds, Fellyn told an inspiring tale of how he had fought the ancient beast tooth and claw, how the monster had knocked away his sword and melted his spear, how the dragon had borne him down and threatened to singe his bones and leave him as nothing more than a white shadow on the hillside. But suddenly, Fellyn would say to his breathless audience, he had felt a large stone beneath him, and picked it up. As the dragon opened his mouth to vent his deadly flame, the prince would exclaim, he heaved the rock deep into the throat of the beast where it blocked the surging flame and turned it inward. Thus, said the prince, Sargon burned himself to death even as he created the Glimmerstone.

Such was his story, and the elves of Aerye, who did not wish it known that they had been hiding, testified to its truth. The story was such a triumphal tale that the High Mountain Elves immediately acclaimed Fellyn as their champion and chosen king.

One would think they chose wisely, for King Fellyn's reign turned out to be the most prosperous time the elves had ever known. It seemed that every year the crops were more bountiful and the hunters more successful. Never had the streams been so filled with trout and salmon. The king's miners found veins of gold and silver where none had been seen before, and the kingdom was at peace. Fellyn himself enjoyed remarkable health and youthful vigor. For forty years the gold of his hair, the green of his eyes, and the spring in his step never faded.

As year upon year passed by, the royal coffers became so full that King Fellyn was faced with an unusual problem: what to do with all the goods, all the gold, all the food that flowed into his treasury? Fellyn consulted his counselors, and the answer seemed simple enough. He instructed the royal architects to design a more massive palace and a bigger treasury. He ordered the master of his grooms to buy more thoroughbred horses and to build larger stables. He commissioned the most talented artists to fill the palace with beauty. He imported new chefs and vintners that his table might be laden with

the best food and wine. On a hillside above the palace, he built a massive tomb to celebrate his triumph, with gem-encrusted dragons
engraved above the entrance.

Elves from all over the world heard of Fellyn's fortune, of course,
and they came to admire his new throne room and to marvel at the
beautiful sculptures of marble and gold. Sometimes the king would
invite visiting dignitaries to his daily feast, but as time passed, he grew
less and less involved in the lives of other people. When problems of
injustice were brought before him, he had little time or patience to
deal with them. When outlying elves who did not share in the king's
good fortune sent emissaries to request assistance for their poor villages, as often as not they were sent back home with empty hands.

The Glimmerstone seemed almost lost in the grandeur of the new
great hall, almost unnoticed in its small, simple niche beside the
throne, almost forgotten, *but now the Glimmerstone was weeping.* The
housekeepers noticed it first. They showed it to the king, who called
upon his wisest sages and most powerful mages, but despite their
dreadful spells, none could stanch the tears of the Glimmerstone.

In time, the elves could see that the Glimmerstone was growing
smaller, and it should come as no surprise to learn that King Fellyn
began to age even as the Glimmerstone began to shrink. The gold
faded from his hair, his eyesight dimmed, and his spine began to
curve. In a matter of weeks, he became a very old man. On the last
day of his mortal life, the king had his servants set what remained of
the Glimmerstone before him and leave him alone with it. He would
not allow anyone to approach, not even his wife, not even his children.

Near the end of the day, even as Fellyn watched, the last of the
quartz dissolved from the stone and all that was left were little flecks of
mica spread darkly across the top of the golden stand. The aging king's
eyes were growing weak as he pondered the sight, but he could see
well enough to realize that the shining flecks had arranged themselves
in the form of a four-letter word, and the word was "FOOL."

When Fellyn's heart stopped beating and he fell from the throne,
the tiny sparkles were scattered across the floor and mingled with the
crystal tears. So it was when the king was laid beneath the dragons in

his tomb, he was the only one who ever knew why the Glimmerstone had wept.

JESUS AND THE RICH FOOL

As far as I know, Jesus never told a single story about an *elfish* man, but he did tell a remarkable story about a *selfish* man who has been remembered ever since as the rich fool. The story began with an incredible harvest so inordinately large that even the wealthy man was amazed. Jesus made a point of saying that "the earth" brought forth his massive harvest. It was a miracle. It was a gift.

And for the rich man, it created an unusual problem—"what to do with it all?" As Jesus told the story, the man didn't really recognize it as a problem. He pondered only briefly before deciding to tear down all of his old barns and build newer, bigger ones.

> And he thought to himself, "What should I do, for I have no place to store my crops?" Then he said, "I will do this: I will pull down my barns and build larger ones, and there I will store all my grain and my goods. And I will say to my soul, 'Soul, you have ample goods laid up for many years; relax, eat, drink, be merry.'" (Luke 12:17-19)

The man never recognized his great blessings as a gift, never acknowledged God as his benefactor. He never considered how he could use that blessing to feed the hungry and shelter the homeless, or to aid poor farmers in danger of losing their ancestral land. The rich man thought only of himself, and so he wastefully tore down his old barns and built bigger and better barns so that his grain and his goods would be secure, his "stuff" would be safe.

But, while his wealth was secure, the man himself was not. Another voice intrudes into the story. It is the voice of God. As Jesus told the story, God came to the man and said, "You fool! This very night your life is being demanded of you. And the things you have prepared, whose will they be?" (v. 20).

We must note that this is not a case of divine capital punishment. God is not saying, "You were greedy, so I will kill you." What the text says, literally, is "*they* will demand your life of you."

And who is "they"?

Could it be his goods? His riches? The rich man thought that he had possessed all his things, but it turned out that his things possessed him, and ultimately they became the end of him.

Jesus' comment was brief: "So it is with those who store up treasures for themselves but are not rich toward God" (Luke 12:21). All of us must answer for the way we have lived our lives.

AFTERTHOUGHTS

This is a hard parable for us to love because most of us would secretly like to be rich, but none of us would like to be called a fool. The truth is that we are not that much different from others in our culture, a culture that is engrossed in having the newest, the biggest, the fastest, the nicest, the "coolest," the most technologically advanced of all things. Many of us know that we have a problem with materialism. We know that we have a hard time deciding where our primary allegiance goes. I suspect we have all tried to worship both God and Mammon, despite Jesus' insistence that it cannot be done (Luke 16:13).

We are blessed beyond measure, but so often we fail to acknowledge that our blessings are from God. Both our political and economic systems now seem to be dominated by those who are the wealthiest. It is endemic in our culture that we seem primarily concerned with how to hold on to our stuff and how to get more. We build bigger barns, bigger houses, bigger bank accounts, bigger retirement funds, and we think they will give us peace of mind, but they do not.

It is not wrong to prepare responsibly for the future, but there is something terribly wrong about living with no sense of responsibility toward others. The parable of the rich fool reminds us that true security and peace is not found in worldly wealth, but in a generous spirit.

Psalm 14:1a uses a familiar word: "A fool says in his heart: there is no God" (author's translation). Whether we *say* there is no God, or just *live as if* there is no God makes little difference. If we acknowledge no transcendent, higher claim upon us and our possessions than our own comfort and pleasure—if we see no connection between our resources and our responsibilities—then we are not unlike the fool who says in his heart, "There is no God: the only one who matters is me."

Jesus had no qualms about calling the rich man—the totally self-centered rich man—a fool. If the Lord were to examine our lives and our living today, and to sum them up in one word, what would that word be?

And when he spoke it, would he be weeping?

NO PRINCE, NO PEACE
Isaiah 9:1-7

THE PRINCE OF MURK AND THE EYE OF THE NEEDLE

There was trouble under the mountain.

There was trouble under the mountain because that is where the dwarves lived, and dwarves are always trouble. When dwarves come to mind, certain words also come to mind; words like irascible or irritable or cantankerous, or touchy or testy or petulant—or just about any synonym for "grumpy." There may be a handful of dwarves who have a spirit of diplomacy about them, but they weren't the ones causing the trouble, of course.

Not that *you* would notice their troubles. You could live out your whole life and not even know that there's such a thing as a dwarf, for they live underground and rarely venture into the outside world.

Have you ever seen one? I rest my case.

Dwarves are distrustful of the open air, and the few entrances that lead into their subterranean home are well disguised and virtually inaccessible to persons so large and clumsy as humans.

The dwarves who lived beneath the Murky Mountains kept mostly to themselves. They didn't like toplanders any more than they liked blue skies and clouds. Then again, they didn't like each other very much, either. This was usually not much of a problem because dwarves tend to mind their own business and ignore each other as much as possible, but sometimes the mountain put their business in the same place.

So it was that the Scarlet Dwarves came into conflict with the Gentian Dwarves, because they both had business in the same deep grotto. The Scarlet Dwarves lived in the lower caverns and gave themselves to mining. They lived to dig and they loved the challenge of tracing narrow veins of gold or silver. They traded raw ore with the Gentian Dwarves, who dwelt in the deepest chambers of the mountain.

The Gentian dwarves worked in steaming pits where lava still flowed, tapping the earth's primeval fires to heat their forges where they smelted the raw ore and shaped it into shining gold and silver bars they would later use to make wondrous things. Throughout the night and day (for dwarves don't notice the difference), the sound of picks and hammers echoed through the darkness as the Scarlet Dwarves coaxed the ore from the rock, and as the Gentian Dwarves worked the precious metal into rings and chains and the most elaborate brooches and pendants. They traded with the Obsidian Dwarves for gemstones, and created jewelry of breathtaking beauty and remarkable delicacy.

It may seem a bit strange to you that creatures who appeared as blunt and crude as the dwarves would have such an eye for beautiful things, but nothing brought them greater joy than to create something shapely and shining to brighten their dark and dusty abode. Then again, nothing angered them more than to have someone else threaten their particular corner of that world.

So, when the Scarlet Dwarves built a dam and diverted the lava flow so they could dig beneath it, the Gentian Dwarves declared war. Negotiating did not occur to them. When dwarves of other tribes got in the way, they dealt with the obstacle the same way they tackled a patch of particularly hard rock. So the Gentian Dwarves set out with picks and hammers to remove the Scarlet Dwarves, and the two groups engaged in an ugly battle that went on for months.

Now, it should be said that there was more bluster than blood involved because the dwarves didn't particularly enjoy dying and harbored no visions of a peaceful afterlife in a perfect underworld. Many more dwarves were captured than killed, but the unpleasantness continued for so long that it began to impact the lives of other tribes, and the High Dwarves of the upper caverns were forced to take notice.

The High Dwarves had ruled the mountain since long before anyone could remember, and their rule had been successful in large part because they rarely meddled in the lives of their subjects. For this reason, they had won the allegiance of the Scarlet Dwarves and the Gentian Dwarves, along with the Taupe Dwarves who farmed the mushrooms, and the Cerulean Dwarves who tended the underground fisheries, and the Russet Dwarves who wove the common dwarfish cloth from fibers they obtained by gathering and drying and pounding roots that grew near the surface.

When the Scarlet Dwarves and the Gentian Dwarves went to war, they no longer had time to mine ore and forge metal, so they could no longer trade for food and clothes with the Taupe and Cerulean and Russet dwarves. The supply of new coins dried up, and the whole underground economy went into a tailspin. The Scarlet and Gentian Dwarves sent out separate raiding parties to steal provisions from the Taupe and Cerulean and Russet dwarves so they could continue to fight each other, and the Cerulean and Russet and Taupe dwarves retaliated with raids of their own. Soon, it became apparent that the High Dwarves would have to get involved, though they might have preferred to sleep in a snake pit.

So it was that King Morgon of the High Dwarves sent royal emissaries to the lower dwarves in hopes of negotiating a peace, but the emissaries came back quickly, missing their shirttails. He sent more senior officials, and they were sent back without their beards, in utter shame.

Finally, Morgon called upon Prince Shallum, who was widely regarded as the most skillful and innovative of his sons, and he sent him out as an ambassador to try to negotiate some kind of peace among the warring factions.

Prince Shallum studied the history of the deep-earth dwarves and examined dusty maps of their nether homelands. Armed only with knowledge and good intent, the prince paid personal visits to the various chieftains of the lower dwarves, and appeared to gain their grudging respect. In time, Prince Shallum persuaded leaders from every level of the mountain to call a temporary truce and meet with him for a summit at the Eye of the Needle.

You may not have heard of the Needle's Eye, but it was well known among the dwarves, and marked on all the maps. The eye was in a vast, forbidding cavern where a rock ledge clung to the outer wall, but the floor dropped sharply into a pit so deep that no one, not even the Gentian Dwarves, had plumbed the full extent of its depths. A bright yellow coating on walls and ceilings, along with the strong smell of sulfur that arose with the hot fumes from the deep, made it obvious that the shaft was an old volcanic vent, and that somewhere below was a pool of bubbling lava.

From the north side of the cavern a slender needle of rock extended from the floor into the pit, so that one could walk out into the middle of the gloomy shaft, where the outcropping widened enough for ten dwarves to stand abreast, but there it stopped.

The Eye of the Needle was the one place Prince Shallum knew where he could isolate the leaders of each party from their followers, so he could be sure there was no treachery. With nothing to protect him but his own good will, the prince led a representative from each of the warring factions to follow him into the cavern, along the narrow walkway, and onto the Eye of the Needle.

When they came to the eye, where the prince had arranged a careful circle of identical chairs, he began to speak. "You have been at war with one another for many months," he said. "Do you understand what this war is doing to our kingdom?" The dwarf leaders nodded their heads. Of course they knew.

The prince pressed on. He talked about the innocent children and the dwarf women that the men rarely saw. He explained the extent of their suffering and uncertainty and even danger. "Wouldn't you like to live in peace again and focus on your work?" the prince asked. With much shifting of eyes and shuffling of feet, each of the dwarves grunted in reluctant assent.

"I know that my beard is not nearly so long as yours," said the prince, and it was true, for the chieftains wore their beards in long braids that were tucked into their belts. Most of them had gone gray and some of them were completely white while the prince's blondish braids hardly reached his chest. "I know that my years may seem as short as my stature to you, but if you want to live in peace," the prince explained in his most diplomatic tone of voice, "you must agree to live by certain rules. You must learn to talk to each other. You must find a way to cooperate with each other. You must agree to compromise when you get in each other's way."

The chieftains of the Scarlet Dwarves and the Gentian Dwarves just scowled at each other, and the leaders of the Cerulean and Russet and Taupe dwarves frowned at the Scarlets and the Gentians. But the prince refused to be discouraged. "There is a better way," he said. "I have come to lay it before you."

The dwarf chieftains grumbled.

"If you want peace," said the prince, "you must learn to respect the king's law and stop taking matters into your own hands. You must let me help you reach a mutual understanding that will respect the rights of all and bring benefits to every tribe."

As he spoke these words, the five dwarf leaders exchanged surreptitious glances and almost imperceptible hand signals. When the prince came to the end of his speech, they nodded in acknowledgment, then moved apart from the prince and huddled together. The prince could hear them grunting quietly in subdued tones, but could not make out their words. He could see them scratching their heads and tugging at their beards and kicking at the dirt as they talked. Occasionally, one of them would turn and look his way.

After a time that seemed much longer than it really was, the five leaders appeared to reach some point of agreement. In one accord, they turned and looked toward the prince, who inwardly congratulated himself for having brought the warring factions together.

As the prince imagined the rewards he might receive and tried not to smile too broadly, the chieftains walked stiffly back to the circle, where they surrounded Shallum's chair. They said not a word, but together they reached out ten strong arms, picked up the prince, and threw him into the yawning chasm.

As the prince's cry of surprise faded away, the chieftains walked back to join their troops, who wasted no time in returning to battle.

The dwarves said they wanted peace, but they did not want the prince. At the end of the day, they had neither.

THE PRINCE OF PEACE AND THE WORLD OF DARKNESS

Many years ago, between the high slopes of Lebanon to the north and west, and the majestic mountains of Moab to the south and east, there existed a nation made of twelve tribes who fought among themselves with all the family pride and personal selfishness they could muster. The people of the nation succeeded quite well in dividing themselves, of course, and then they fell into the perpetual danger of being conquered by other nations more powerful than they.

The Creator and High King of this nation sent prophetic messengers to these people, one after the other, in hopes that they might hear of a better way and listen to reason and regain a sense of peace. Often they ran these prophets out of town. Sometimes they threw them into mud pits, or put them in prison, or stoned them. The people were so caught up in their own quarrels and their own misguided notions that they refused to hear any words of warning or of peace.

Yet, the Lord of this nation Israel continued to send his messengers, and one of them was named Isaiah. To Isaiah the High King entrusted a promise that seemed quite out of place, for in the midst of war, it promised peace:

> But there will be no gloom for those who were in anguish. In the former time he brought into contempt the land of Zebulun and the land of Naphtali, but in the latter time he will make glorious the way of the sea, the land beyond the Jordan, Galilee of the nations.
> The people who walked in darkness have seen a great light; those who lived in a land of deep darkness—on them light has shined.
> You have multiplied the nation, you have increased its joy; they rejoice before you as with joy at the harvest, as people exult when dividing plunder.
> For the yoke of their burden, and the bar across their shoulders, the rod of their oppressor,

you have broken as on the day of Midian.
For all the boots of the tramping warriors and all the garments
rolled in blood
shall be burned as fuel for the fire.
For a child has been born for us, a son given to us;
authority rests upon his shoulders;
and he is named Wonderful Counselor, Mighty God,
Everlasting Father, Prince of Peace.
His authority shall grow continually, and there shall be endless
peace
for the throne of David and his kingdom.
He will establish and uphold it with justice and with right-
eousness
from this time onward and forevermore.
The zeal of the Lord of hosts will do this.

What a beautiful promise.

What an incredible piece of poetry.

What a waste of breath!

A waste, at least, as far as Isaiah's listeners were concerned. They were not ready to accept the High King's way, were not willing to acknowledge any Prince of Peace, and they spent the rest of their days in conflict.

But that is not the end of the story.

A little more than 700 years after Isaiah foretold the birth of this great Savior of Israel, there was born to the High King a son. The child was called "Jesus," and at his birth the angels sang and declared peace on earth.

Jesus grew up and lived among his people and when the appropriate time came, he began to teach them what it meant to live at peace with God and in peace with one another. He taught them to love each other and to consider the needs of others before their own. He called on them to acknowledge the law of the Kingdom of God, and to follow in the way of the King.

In response, the people of Jesus' day put their heads together, put their arms out, picked up the Prince of Peace, and nailed him to a cross.

They wanted peace, but not the Prince. When all was said and done, they had neither.

THE PRINCE OF PEACE AND YOU

By now, you may be thinking, "Your imaginary dwarves are just stupid. The Israelites were stupid. The people of Jesus' day were stupid. They ought to know better than that."

But what I want to ask you is this: "Do you want peace in *your* life?"

Do you *really* want peace?

Have you found it?

Sadly, many who say they want peace do not have it, and often that is because we are still trying to find peace without the Prince.

What we must understand is this: the peace of Christ does not come without the presence of Christ. There are many of us who give lip service to the idea of living in peace with God and at peace with one another, yet we live in inner turmoil and outer conflict. Our insides are stressed and our relationships are stretched. We long for peace, but don't find it.

Could it be that we want the peace without the Prince? The Scriptures teach us that we can have peace with God—but that peace comes through following Christ: "Therefore, since we are justified by faith, we have peace with God through our Lord Jesus Christ" (Rom 5:1). If we want to know the peace of God, we need to know the Prince of God's plan. We need to know Jesus.

Jesus has promised peace for this world's struggles and peace that stretches beyond this world. In his last extended conversation with the disciples, according to John's Gospel, Jesus explained that he would always be present with them through his Spirit, leading and guiding and giving comfort. "Peace I leave with you," he said, "my peace I give to you. I do not give as the world gives. Do not let your hearts be troubled, and do not let them be afraid" (John 14:27). "I have said this to you," he concluded later, "so that in me you may have peace. In this world you will face tribulation, but I have overcome the world" (John 16:33).

In these amazing words, Jesus promised his own presence in our lives, the presence of a divine Prince who offers inner peace. Take note that one does not come without the other. You cannot have peace without the Prince! It is Christ's presence that offers peace.

It is important for us to look again at the beginning of the marvelous speech that promised peace, because we need to understand that Christ's presence in us is not automatic. His Spirit will not dwell where he is not welcome, or in a heart that is not prepared.

In John 14:15-17, Jesus says, "If you love me, you will keep my commandments. And I will ask the Father, and he will give you another Advocate, to be with you forever. This is the Spirit of truth, whom the world cannot receive, because it neither sees him nor knows him. You know him, because he abides with you, and he will be in you."

Christ abides in the hearts of those who love him, and he defines those who love him as those who keep his commandments, who follow his way, who live the life of unselfish love that Jesus set out as an example to us. The Spirit of Christ, the Spirit of Love, and the Spirit of Peace are all interconnected.

There is no peace without the Prince.

> **Author's note:** This reflection was inspired by a quotation from Addison Leitch, in Christianity Today, 22 December 1972. There, Leitch said, "Our trouble is we want the peace without the prince."

FOLLOWING HOPE

John 14:1-14

FOLLOWING HOPE

When Boone Sampson and his friend Gloria wandered off by themselves, they didn't intend to stay gone for very long. But they didn't intend to find themselves in an enchanted forest, either.

Things happen.

The two friends had come to the forest with their youth group from Amity Glen Baptist Church. The summer youth director had concocted a day of activities at Broad River Park, where he led the high schoolers through an obstacle course in hopes of building fellowship and team spirit.

As the organized activities ended and the parent chaperones started getting supper together beneath a rented picnic shelter, the tired teens were granted a bit of free time. That was just the opening Boone was looking for. He had been wanting to get better acquainted with Gloria Smalley, and he persuaded her to take a walk with him after they helped ice down the soft drinks and collect some firewood.

With permission from one of the adult leaders, they walked through a broad meadow by the river, picking their way along spotty trails left by hikers before them. As they ambled downstream, however, the riverbank grew increasingly muddy and soft, so they turned toward higher ground.

Boone had been a Boy Scout, so every now and then he would take note of some landmark or keep an eye on the sun so they could find their way back to the others. They didn't worry too much, though. When Gloria said something about how far from the shelter they had come, Boone calmed her nerves. "All we have to do is go back downhill toward the river," he said, "then walk back upstream to the park."

As they climbed uphill from the valley bottom, a band of thick vegetation and scrub oaks gave way to a beautifully open pine forest, where the two friends collapsed on the soft and fragrant carpet of pine needles to share some trail mix and water. They stretched out and watched the treetops dancing in the breeze beneath cottony clouds, bowing to their partners as the birds kept time.

They could have stayed there all day, just the two of them, sharing newfound secrets and breathing the fresh forest air and watching Mother Nature dance. But the young friends knew they needed to get back. The other youth would be wondering what they were up to, and their adult leaders would be worried if they didn't return soon. They helped each other up and walked back through the enchanting pine forest to rejoin their friends.

Enjoying the prickly, goose-bumpy tingle of holding hands for the first time, Boone and Gloria hiked down the hill to where the scrub oaks again infringed upon the pines, and they pushed on through the heavier undergrowth for longer than they expected, but they couldn't seem to find the river. "We must have gotten turned around," Boone said, "and walked down the wrong side of the hill." Gloria wasn't so sure, but they couldn't come up with any better explanation. They did an about-face to head back toward the open forest, but they couldn't seem to find the tall pines, either. Every twist and turn led them deeper into the scruffy oaks and entangling vines.

The sun was beginning its long slide to the western horizon, but the sky had become so overcast that Boone and Gloria could not make out its direction anymore. The air on every side seemed to take on something of an eerie glow, as if the humidity was charged with electricity. Tree frogs began their sundown serenade, and a screech owl called in the distance, and Gloria began to cry softly. Boone yelled as loudly as he could, hoping that the other youth would answer and guide them back, but only the bullfrogs returned his call.

The friends pushed ahead in the gathering dusk, heading slightly downhill in what they thought must be the right direction, growing more frantic by the minute, when they came upon an unmistakable pathway through the underbrush. They didn't remember crossing a path before, but decided that it had to lead *somewhere*, so they turned in the direction that seemed most downhill and followed the trail into the growing darkness. Gloria and Boone held tightly to each other, for soon they could see the path only in moonlight. Every now and then one of them would stop and listen, thinking perhaps that they had heard someone from the group calling their names, then deciding it was just the wind in the trees.

It was Gloria who first noticed a flickering light ahead, and soon they stumbled into a small clearing occupied by a tiny cabin made of logs, with a roof of woven rushes and a candle glowing through the open door. "Hello!" they both called. "Is anybody home? Hello!"

No one answered. Boone and Gloria were too polite to go inside the cabin without an invitation, so they wandered about the small clearing while speculating about just who would live in such an out-of-the-way place. Boone insisted it was probably some disgruntled man who had taken up the hermit's life for reasons known only to himself, but Gloria was thinking of Snow White and Hansel and Gretel, and she wondered if the neat little cabin might belong to a mean old witch. Boone was tempted to laugh at such an idea, but he wanted to stay in Gloria's good graces, so he held his tongue.

In any case, both of them were startled when they heard someone singing from another path on the far side of the cabin, for the voice was not that of a crotchety hermit or a wicked witch. No, the voice clearly belonged to a young woman, and her lilting song was like the scent of a rose on a morning in May. The shimmering melody floated through the darkness and wrapped itself around Gloria and Boone while the singer followed behind. They were standing together, mesmerized, when a slender woman appeared around the corner and sang her way across the clearing until she stood before her new guests. She appeared not the least surprised to find them there.

"Hello, Gloria!" she said softly. "Hello, Boone." Before the two friends could stammer out a response or ask how she knew their names, she said, "Won't you come inside and share some bread? I'm sure you are hungry by now." Without a word, the dumbfounded pair followed her into the cabin, sat on two wooden stools, and watched as their hostess found a small loaf of bread and divided it between them. They had hundreds of questions, but somehow it seemed inappropriate to ask them.

Who are you? they wondered. And *Why do you live in the woods?* And *Where did you learn how to make such marvelous bread?* All these things and more they thought, of course, but they held their peace because their host was humming such a comforting tune that neither of them wanted to interrupt. Somehow they could see in the young woman's eyes that she already knew all of their questions, and she would tell them what they needed to know, but in her own time.

Boone thought to himself that he had never seen anyone who went barefoot stay so clean and neat, while Gloria wondered if the woman had woven the simple tunic she wore. It looked something like burlap, though softer, and its light brown color matched her hair that was cut short and hugged her ears.

The woodland woman joined Boone and Gloria at the table just as they finished eating, and her humming faded away. Gloria began to explain that they were lost, and in a torrent of words she told her the whole story, and when she finished she was crying again. Boone wept, too, but he succeeded in keeping the tears on the inside.

The lady smiled just a little, and her eyes seemed to sparkle a bit more than before. "Oh, set your hearts at ease," she said. "I know where your friends are, with their cars and their campfires and their supper cooking on the coals. I know. Don't worry—they'll save some for you, and you'll be there soon. You know the way."

Boone blurted out a confession that they were lost. "What are you talking about?" he asked. "We couldn't find our way out of these woods even in daylight, and now it is dark. How can you say that we know the way to get back? Can you show us a path that will take us there?"

The woman smiled again, though faintly, and her voice was like sunshine on snow. "Oh, no," she said. "There is no path through these woods. You won't even find the one that brought you here, for it existed just for a while, just for that purpose. I can't give you a list of rules or directions, for it would be more than you could remember, and more than you could do. If I send you out alone you'll just wind up in the mud again, and there's quicksand out there, too. But you can get back. You know the way."

Now Gloria was getting perplexed. "What do you mean? We're helpless and hopeless in these swampy old woods! We'll never find our way out! How can you say that we know the way?"

"Because you know *me*," said the woman, and her smile was infectious. "You know me. You won't get back, except by me, and that's the truth. But I will not fail you. I am your way home. Follow me, and I will take you where you need to go."

The woman then pulled a light hood over her head and walked out of the warm cabin, into the evening mist. Boone and Gloria scrambled to follow. "Ma'am?" Boone asked. "What if we get separated and need to call you? Will you tell us your name?"

"Of course I will," she called back from somewhere in the darkness. "You can call me 'Hope,' and you can call me anytime."

Following Jesus

On a dark night in Jerusalem, the rabbi Jesus gathered with a group of his friends in a room, sharing a simple meal of bread and wine. Twelve men were gathered around him—Jewish men who sought truth and enlightenment, men who had adopted him as their rabbi some years before. Month after month, Jesus had taught them things that would never have come into their heads if not for him. The young rabbi gave them new insights into the law of Israel, and into the heart of God, and into the life of his people. Their lives were enriched beyond measure just by being with him.

Lately, though, their teacher had been acting strange. He had been talking about leaving them. They were worried sick, and Jesus knew it. So, he spoke to them. Calmly. Yet forcefully. He said,

"Do not let your hearts be troubled. Trust in God; trust also in me. In my Father's house are many rooms; if it were not so, I would have told you. I am going there to prepare a place for you. And if I go and prepare a place for you, I will come back and take you to be with me that you also may be where I am. You know the way to the place where I am going."

Thomas said to him, "Lord, we don't know where you are going, so how can we know the way?"

Jesus answered, "I am the way and the truth and the life. No one comes to the Father except through me. If you really knew me, you would know my Father as well. From now on, you do know him and have seen him." (John 14:1-7, NIV)

Jesus said far more that day than his disciples ever expected to hear, but less than they really wanted to hear. He made promises that went beyond all human hopes, but the disciples may have thought he left them with more riddles than answers.

Jesus spoke of a home in heaven with the Father—a house with many rooms, an eternal dwelling already prepared for the children of God. He spoke as if the disciples already knew where it was and how to get there, but they didn't have a clue.

Don't you wish you knew where heaven was? That you had some empirical proof that it really does exist in space and time? That someone could give you directions like "follow Kildaire Farm Road to Maynard Road and turn right"? Those are the kind of directions Thomas was looking for when he was the only one willing to speak up and admit, "Lord, we don't know where you are going, so how can we know the way?"

That is why Jesus responded by smiling, I am sure, and by saying, "*I* am the way." You don't get to heaven by following a road map. You get there by following Jesus. The way to the Father, the way to the Father's eternal home, runs right through Jesus. Through Jesus, who is often misunderstood and sometimes a bit confusing to us, but always reaching out to those who are looking for the way home.

Jesus is the way, the truth, and the life. If we think we've got him all figured out, that is sure evidence that we've lost our way in the swamp. We follow a Lord who is always out there ahead of us, a Lord we can't always see, but in whom we can hope—one who is always available to us, always willing to hear our cry.

We follow a Lord who calls us to follow him by living as he lives, by loving others unselfishly, by trusting in the presence of his Spirit to lead us in the right way. We may often feel lost in this sinful, selfish world, separated from friends and family and God as well. But we are never so lost that Jesus cannot find us, never so far away that he cannot hear us when we call, never so desolate that we do not have *hope* in knowing that there *is* a way, and that we know the way, because we know Jesus—and more importantly, we have assurance that Jesus knows *us*.

GROWING STONES
GATHER NO MOSS

1 Peter 2:1-12

THE CHURCH OF THE LIVING STONES

A long time ago, in a land far away, a rustic village nestled against the edge of a royal wood near the outer reaches of the Kingdom of Kent. The village was called Bundletown because of the many bundles of hay stacked throughout the fields that surrounded the hamlet and fed its cows. The town itself had only a few streets arranged around a central plaza that was covered with grass. There was a decrepit inn or two, and a smattering of dry goods shops. Most people grew their own groceries or went to the common green on Saturdays for market day and bartered with their neighbors. On Sundays they *all* went to church.

Bundletown was an unassuming place, and its people were known for their simplicity of life and depth of faith. They grieved, however, because their church building was falling down. Bundletonians worshiped in a small chapel built of ancient logs that leaned in the wind and gave way to the rain. They longed for a new building to give outward testimony of their quiet faith and their strident love for God, but the king would not allow any wood to be cut from the royal forest, and stones were rare in that part of the world.

So it was that the church was old, and the town buildings were old, and the thatched-roof cottages scattered along the village streets were old, and there was little hope of repairing them. Bundletown was close to becoming a bundle of sticks, and it seemed that no one in all the Kingdom of Kent cared anything for the people's plight.

The village priest in Bundletown was a rather young man, but he was immensely popular, for he loved the people and served them well. He had dark hair and a plain, open face with a winning smile, and his voice was as smooth and comforting as a mountain stream. For many years he had served as the old priest's acolyte, but when the aged man could no longer carry the smoking censer or remember the prayers, his young disciple had taken over. The young priest's name was Gwynn, and despite his youth, all the people called him "Father."

Gwynn was burdened for the people of Bundletown, and he prayed earnestly for them, for it seemed the poor village had no future. But it seemed that his prayers brought no rain to help the crops, no royal visitors with grants of gold to help the village.

There came a day when Gwynn hiked alone in the royal forest, as he often did, and he prayed a walking prayer, as was his custom. Deep in the wood that day, as Gwynn's whispered meditation marked the time to his steady walk, there came to him a vision of something so astonishing that he fell to his knees beneath an ancient oak and struggled to catch his breath. The hanging moss from the massive tree made for an impressive outdoor cathedral, but the image in Gwynn's mind was of something no one had seen before. He knelt for a while and prayed that the vision might be so, and he felt as if the Lord had touched him with a special power that could make his vision live.

Later that day, when the mayor of Bundletown looked up from his rickety desk and saw the priest standing before him with dirt on his knees and bits of moss in his hair, he was not surprised, for they visited often, and everyone knew Gwynn went to the wood to pray. But there was something different in the young man's eyes, something alive, something that twinkled, something that shouted for attention.

"Mayor Wolden," Gwynn said, "God has given to me a vision of something that could be the salvation of our church and our village—

and he has shown me how it might come to pass. I propose that we build a majestic new cathedral right on the village green!"

The mayor just looked at Gwynn, for he was certain that the young priest knew all woodcutting was forbidden and stones were hard to find. He waited for the other shoe to fall, and it quickly did. "Friend Mayor, I know you are thinking to yourself that I have lost my senses, for we have no building materials save bundles of hay, and that is hardly good for thatching a roof, and cannot be used to build a cathedral.

"Here is my plan, Mayor Wolden—a plan straight from the Scriptures. Do you remember the Apostle Peter, and did you remember that his real name was Simon, but that Jesus called him 'Peter' because *petros* means 'rock,' and Jesus said, 'Upon this rock I will build my church'? You do remember? I thought you would.

"And do you remember that this same Peter wrote a letter to the early churches of Asia Minor, and in that letter he said, 'Come to him, a living stone, though rejected by mortals yet chosen and precious in God's sight, and like living stones, let yourselves be built into a spiritual house, to be a holy priesthood, to offer spiritual sacrifices acceptable to God through Jesus Christ'?" (1 Pet 2:4-5)

The mayor nodded briefly through knotted brows, as he wondered where all of this would lead. When Gwynn stepped closer and spoke earnestly in hushed tones, the mayor's eyes grew wide with disbelief, but so persuasive was the young priest that Mayor Wolden agreed to let him try.

So it was that on the following Sunday the villagers packed into the old leaning church, as they always did, and they sang off key, as they always did, and they sat down for the homily, as they always did. But, when Father Gwynn threw back his hood to preach, as he always did, there was magic in his eyes.

He preached that day as he had spoken earlier to the mayor. He reminded the people of their great devotion to God and of their fruitless existence on the fringes of the kingdom. He challenged them to do something remarkable and impressive for the glory of God and the good of their village. He challenged those who were willing to give themselves in God's service to come to Christ like living stones, and let themselves be built into the true church of God.

As soon as the benediction was sung, Father Gwynn marched from the sagging church to the village green, and one by one, some more eagerly than others, his congregation followed him there. When all were gathered, Gwynn called out the oldest members of the church, a man and a woman, and brought them to the center of the lawn. Under his direction, they faced each other and knelt, and then reached out their arms and locked them together. When they put their heads down in prayer, they looked almost like a low table, and as the young priest began to chant and wave his hands over their backs, an amazing thing began to happen.

The arms of the man and the woman became firm and still. Soon there was no movement in their bodies at all. Someone noticed that their feet were taking on a grey cast, and gradually the color spread until it covered their bodies as the two together became one living stone in the shape of an altar carved to appear as two people kneeling in eternal prayer.

The people were still gasping in astonishment as the young priest joyously called out one name after another until he had arranged every man in the village into the shape of a rectangle surrounding the altar, leaving only enough space for a door.

Mimicking the shape he would have them take, he instructed each man to stand with feet spread apart and hands held high so that they touched the feet and gripped the hands of their neighbor. In unison, the men lifted their heads and offered praise to God as Father Gwynn danced about the rectangle, chanting his prayers and dodging in and out of the line of men.

Soon it was clear to all that the men's hands were molding together and growing flat on top, and their feet were reaching deep into the soft ground. Together, the men of Bundletown became as one solid wall, a firm foundation. Again the color of slate made its way from feet to hands, and the men were frozen in living stone with beatific expressions of joy on their faces.

Even before the last of the men had become solid, young Gwynn was instructing the women to climb up and stand on the men's hands, making a second row and raising the walls even higher. As the women settled into place and joined their hands and lifted them high, they began to sing, and as they did so the flesh of their bodies welded together and the rustle of their heavy skirts became quiet as they solidified into stone, but even though their lips quickly hardened into expressions of delight, the sound of their singing softly hung in the air.

The priest quickly called out to the children, "Don't you like to climb? Have you ever made a pyramid?" And he led them then to climb up the walls that their parents had made, and on top of each narrow side they made a pyramid, and on the long sides they stood on each other's shoulders until they were just a little taller than the pyramid on either end. As Father Gwynn danced about and pointed and shouted from below, the children felt themselves growing together, growing stronger, growing firm, and those on the long sides allowed themselves to fall inward toward each other until they met in the middle and joined their hands, and as the color of stone crept over them the new cathedral had its roof.

Now, of course, the only thing moving was the priest, and he quickly went to the altar and knelt behind it. There he looked toward heaven with a gratified smile. Holding his hands high with palms uplifted and fingers spread, he continued his chant until his own transformation from living flesh to living stone left him there in the form of the happiest pulpit you have ever seen.

It was a wandering merchant, come to sell his wares on market day, who first saw what had happened. From the outskirts of town he had noticed nothing different. No one was tending the cows, but cows don't take much tending once milking time is over. The buildings he saw were as ramshackle as ever, but, when he came to the village green, there stood the most incredible thing he had ever seen.

Here was something both new and old—here was an open-air church built of stones all carved in the shape of men and women and children. As he walked inside and felt the wonder of the place, the peddler marveled at the beauty of the carving and the expressions of such intense joy that beamed from walls and ceiling alike. He began to inspect the walls more closely, and as he felt the rough beard of one mighty pillar, it suddenly came to him—he recognized this man! And then he saw another, and another—and there was even a carving that looked like the mayor, just beyond that extraordinary pulpit and altar. He had never seen or heard of stonemasons as talented as this.

In the quietness of the moment, the merchant realized that it was not quite as quiet as he had thought, for *he could hear the sound of breathing.* Just a faint breath, not something you would notice at first, but it was there. And, when he turned his head a certain way, he could swear that he heard the sound of women's voices raised in song. Something here was alive.

When the peddler rushed out to question the village people about this marvelous new wonder, there was no one to ask, not a soul to be found. The merchant sat down on the porch of the old inn to ponder what he had seen, and what he had sensed. Remembering that he had recognized some of the stone carvings inside, and the detail on their faces, the peddler came to the inevitable conclusion that someone had enchanted the entire town. Every person in Bundletown was now a part of the most beautiful church that was ever built.

As you might imagine, the traveling salesman left immediately and began a journey to the king's palace, not even trying to peddle his goods along the road. As he passed through towns and hamlets on the way, he told them about the living church, and long before the king heard the news, pilgrims were already making long and difficult journeys to see this marvel. Soon the name "Bundletown" was almost forgotten, but everyone in the kingdom knew about "the Breathing Cathedral."

For the better part of a year, the church remained as it was. The king relaxed his decree and sent in royal loggers and carpenters to rebuild the inns so pilgrims would have a place to stay, and to rebuild the houses in honor of the people who had given themselves to build such a cathedral to the glory of God. They even rebuilt the old leaning church, because it had also become a shrine, and it was made strong and safe for pilgrims to visit.

The Breathing Cathedral became known as the holiest place in all the kingdom, so when the Lenten season came, the king made plans for himself and his family to make a pilgrimage and to worship there on Easter Sunday. Many others had made the same journey, but they held back as the royal family and their personal priest marched through the morning dew and into the church, where they knelt on the soft, green grass. As the early sunlight filtered through the open walls of the cathedral, the king could see the various faces of children and women and men highlighted by the sun, and he was overcome by the commitment of people who would give themselves so completely to the cause of Christ, and by the joy that lined their faces.

He remarked aloud that it was truly miraculous for such a thing to take place, for people to give themselves as living stones to create such a marvelous cathedral. But even as he said this, the king's daughter, who was short in years but long in wisdom, said, "This place is truly beautiful, Father, and the commitment of these people is so impressive. I can't help but think of what a miracle it would be if people could show such faith in their everyday lives."

As the young woman's words hung in the air, a shaft of sunlight fell upon the pulpit, and there was a loud cracking sound. It seemed as if the smile on the young priest's face spread even broader, and everyone turned to see. As the royal family watched, the Easter sunlight seemed to melt away the gray on Gwynn's frozen image. Color crept into his face and hands, and the gray faded from his worn white tunic, and soon the gold cross around his neck was glittering in the morning sun.

Father Gwynn leapt to his feet as if he had only knelt for a moment, and he exclaimed, "Oh, my lady, you have declared a true vision of the great and living church!" And with that, he began to sing and chant in different words, and the gray ceiling of children became a riot of color and movement. "Help me!" shouted the priest, as he began to catch the giggling children who rained down from their former places in the roof and into the arms of those below, including the royal family. Soon the walls regained their color, too, and exuberant families were reunited, and someone helped the elderly couple who had formed the altar to their feet.

The young priest laughed and cried loudly to gain their attention, and he said, "My friends, you have seen the power of God in you. You have watched from wall and ceiling as thousands of pilgrims came here and looked on in wonder that men and women and children would give themselves as living stones in God's service. Now this young princess has come to remind us that our real mission is to be living stones in the real world, showing others not only the joy and the beauty of Christ, but also the warm touch of his love!"

And on that day the people returned to their rebuilt houses, and from that day they worshipped in their wooden church, and every day they lived with a special light in their eyes and a singular love in their hearts. They renamed their church "The Church of the Living Stones," and even though the Breathing Cathedral was gone, pilgrims still came to Bundletown, just to be among people who so lived out their faith. Some of those who had once been stone went out into surrounding villages to proclaim the joy of Christ and to challenge others to hear his call to put away their hypocrisy and to grow up into the faith that God has prepared for his children as a church of living stones.

LIVING STONES

How wonderful and warming it is to imagine a people who truly accept their calling as *a chosen race, a royal priesthood, a holy nation,* knowing that they are *God's own people,* called to *proclaim the mighty acts of God who had called them out of darkness and into his marvelous light.*

Like the people of Bundletown, the words of an apostle named "Rocky" challenge us to a life as living stones. We know that when he calls us to be pillars of the church, it is not as unmoving masonry, but as living stones, loving Christ in our daily lives.

TELLING SECRETS

Ephesians 3:1-13

THE MYSTERY OF KASHIMARI

In the land of Kashimari, there were people who were both handsome and homely, indolent and industrious, wealthy and woeful, but the only thing that really mattered was whether one was born a Skylock or a Scrunge. People outside the isolated mountain kingdom could see no difference, but deep in the shadows of the Simmentall Mountains, it was a matter of life and death.

It was a matter of life and death because the Skylock people were the conservators and beneficiaries of the magical Mystic Manna, which they called the Bread of Life. Every New Year's Eve, at the Feast of the New Beginnings, all the Skylocks in the land of Kashimari would gather by their clans in the great courtyard outside the Temple of Kash. There they would chant the Litany of Hope for a prosperous year, and from the temple would come forth priests both male and female, distributing to each Skylock one palm-sized piece of the Mystic Manna. After joining again in reciting the Litany of Life, each person would eat the Bread of Life with faith that its magical ingredients would feed the life spirit within them and bring them one step closer to the Land of All Things Green.

From ancient days, only the wisest of the oldest women of the Skylock people were entrusted with the secret recipe for mixing and proofing and baking the Mystic Manna, and they never passed the magical formula on to the next generation until they were ready to begin their own journey to the Land of All Things Green. The journey to this eternal land began, so the Skylocks believed, when the life spirit curled itself into a ball within the human shell, leaving the body lifeless and, to all appearances, dead. On the very day in which this happened, family members were required to bring the human shell to the Temple of Kash, where attendants would usher them through a heavy iron door set deep in the great stone walls.

On this day only, on the Day of the Journey In, were ordinary people allowed to enter the abode of the priests. Once inside, they would see a sacred sanctuary much smaller than expected, and a few modest buildings designed to accommodate the priestly families. Beyond these, the temple walls opened onto a great field dotted with rounded boulders. The priests would find a spot where no stone had ever stood, and there they would dig a round hole just a few feet deep. Then, with care, they would curl the human shell into a fetal position, wrap it in a sheet, and gently lower it into the hole before rolling a large rounded stone on top of the new doorway into the earth. The priests and the family would then join hands around the boulder and sing the Song of the Journey, trusting that sound of their song would signal the balled up spirit of life to leave the human shell so that it might be swallowed up by the earth and brought to one of the many subterranean pathways that led to the Land of All Things Green.

That land, as everyone knew, was on the other side of the earth, and it took many days for the rolling spirit to get there, and only a life spirit that had been sufficiently strengthened by the Mystic Manna could hope to survive the journey and emerge safely into the Land of All Things Green, where nothing ever died, and where no evil ever came.

So it was that the Skylocks were prone to look down their noses a bit when considering the Scrunges, because the Skylock people alone had been entrusted with the Mystic Manna and thus the means to find eternal happiness in the Land of All Things Green. Oh, the Scrunges also buried their dead in round holes, and they covered their graves with rolling stones, and they also sang, but since they had no access to the Bread of Life, they had far less hope of surviving the journey.

Now, if you or I happened to stumble upon the deep valley kingdom of Kashimari, the differences between the Skylocks and the Scrunges would be hardly noticeable. Although each group imagined themselves to be more physically attractive than the other, the truth is that you would see no difference at all. Indeed, the only sign of variation you would see is something you would first have to learn, and that is that the Skylocks kept only sheep in their flocks, while the Scrunges kept both sheep and goats.

The Scrunges knew goat meat to be tasty and goat milk to be healthful, but the Skylocks considered the dappled billies and nannies to be second-class animals that were hardly fit to share the same pasture with the beautiful snow-white sheep of Kashimari. They took offense that the Scrunges would allow such animals to live among them, and they took this as an obvious symbol of the Scrunges' general obtuseness of spirit.

It was no wonder, they thought, that the ancient gods of Kash had entrusted the secret of the Mystic Manna to Skylocks alone. They had no desire to associate with the Scrunges and kept themselves segregated as much as possible. Even so, both Skylocks and Scrunges did business together when it was profitable, and they worked together on projects that were mutually beneficial, and the young ones who didn't know any better often played together. But, when it came to issues of intermarriage or sharing the Mystic Manna, the lines were tightly and intractably drawn.

For their part, the Scrunges weren't so sure that the Skylocks had any real advantage, though one could never be certain. Most of the Scrunges secretly longed to be admitted to the Skylock tribe so they could partake of the Bread of Life, but there seemed to be no way such a remarkable thing could take place.

That is how it was in the land of Kashimari—at least until the Lady Myra became the oldest living woman among the Skylocks, and the secret of the Mystic Manna was passed to her through the parched lips of her dying predecessor. As the Lady Myra leaned close and stored the recipe away in her mind, she was overcome by a sudden inspiration. She felt as if an invisible hand from the earth itself had reached up to squeeze her heart. It held her tightly for so long that her attendants began to worry, and when it turned her loose she fell weakly to the ground, but with a distinct and new idea that she perceived as a new revelation from the ancient gods.

As the other priestesses helped Lady Myra to her feet, she announced to those who stood about that she had been gifted with a divine secret, one long hidden but now to be revealed. Without ceremony, she sent them forth to gather all the Skylocks together, even though the Feast of New Beginnings was still several weeks away. Being sole keeper of the secret of the Mystic Manna gave Lady Myra considerable influence, and so the people gathered according to her instructions, awaiting the new revelation. What could it be? Would it be good news or bad? Would it be something that mattered to everyone, or just an arcane religious matter that no one outside of priestly circles would care about?

As the people gathered anxiously outside the temple gate, the new high priestess climbed to the top of the broad stone wall so that she could sit in her large wooden chair, but still see and be seen while speaking. When all was in place, she motioned for silence and began her proclamation in a voice that was ragged at the edges, but strong enough for all to hear.

"A great mystery has been revealed to me," she said. "It is a mystery never known in previous generations, but now I declare it to you. I am not the strongest among you, and perhaps not the wisest. I am, however, the oldest, and the spirit of Kash has come from the earth to grant me a vision of what is to be." The crowd began to murmur, growing impatient for Lady Myra to get on with it and speak her piece.

Finally, the old woman pushed against the arms of her chair and stood as erect as her bent spine would allow, and the mass of people grew silent before her. "This is the secret," she declared, "this is the eternal mystery of the ages now revealed to the Skylocks of Kashimari—Kash has willed that the gift of Mystic Manna and the way to the Land of All Things Green shall belong to Scrunges as well as to Skylocks: the Bread of Life is the inheritance of every person who lives! From this day, there shall be no more Skylock, no more Scrunge, but all shall be one people, serving each other and serving the gods.”

An astounded hush fell over the crowd. Accept the Scrunges? Share the Mystic Manna with Scrunges? Become one with the Scrunges? Surely not! *Surely not!* The crowd began to shout its displeasure, but the Lady Myra motioned once again for quiet, and spoke as loudly as she could: “Here is the will of the gods: not only are the Skylocks to accept the Scrunges, but it is your gift and your glory to carry the word to every village and bring them with you to the great Feast of New Beginnings, that they may share in the Bread of Life! Bring them in! Bring them in!”

Lady Myra’s hope of a new day was short-lived, for her call to revival soon dissolved into a riot. There were shouts of disapproval, and some of the most vocal people began to throw stones along with their words, but Lady Myra stood fast. As the crowd turned into a mob, however, a tree near the courtyard was chopped down and stripped of its branches, then lifted by a hundred hands and used to knock Lady Myra from her chair. Angry Skylocks cut more trees and used them like ladders. They swarmed over the wall and broke Lady Myra’s wooden throne into pieces and marched around the temple grounds with angry fists in the air.

In their rage, however, the people failed to remember that Lady Myra was the only person who had known the secret of the Mystic Manna, and when a faithful priestess found her body crushed beneath the trampling feet, her life spirit had already curled within her, and Lady Myra was left as a human shell, and the Skylocks were left without the knowledge they needed to make the Mystic Manna, even for themselves.

Did any of the people who threw her down stop to consider that such action might jeopardize their own future life? Perhaps, but if so, it was a chance they were willing to take, for the Skylocks believed it was better to die on the path to the Land of All Things Green than to share that land with a Scrunge.

THE MYSTERY OF THE CHURCH

That, as you know, was a tall tale. Nothing in it was really true except the human nature it revealed. But here is another story. One that *is* true. One that is *too* true. There was a time when it could be said that all the peoples of the known world were divided into two groups of people: the Jews and the Gentiles. The Bible declares that the true God of all had called the Jews to be God's special people and had blessed them in various ways through many years. The Jews of first-century Palestine were proud to be inheritors of the ancient tradition and the gatekeepers of eternity. It was not impossible for Gentiles to get there, but they had to swear off their past and deny their heritage and become Jews in order to do it.

A time came, however, when the Spirit of God spoke through a man named Jesus and declared that God's love was for all peoples. Jesus taught that sincere faith in God was more important than following ancient rituals. He called upon the Jewish people of his day to accept this new revelation of God and to accept Gentile believers into their family. In response, according to the Gospels, they arranged for his execution.

Some years later, an activist Jewish rabbi named Saul set himself to the task of arresting everyone he could find who still followed the way of that crucified teacher. But, as Saul traveled the road to Damascus in search of more potential prisoners, the Spirit of God reached out and grabbed his heart and would not let him go. Jesus himself appeared to Saul in a blinding vision on the road to Damascus. He challenged Saul not only to trust in him, but to spend the rest of his life reaching out to the very persons he once had hated: he was to become an apostle to the Gentiles.

Saul's name was changed to Paul as a symbol of his new identity, and the Bible declares that he committed himself to that calling with the same zeal that characterized his earlier attacks. Saul endured many sufferings and persecutions to proclaim the gospel among the same Gentiles he had once despised.

Saul was given a great vision of bringing reconciliation between all of God's people. In his efforts to do so, Paul decided to travel throughout Asia Minor and collect an offering from the Gentile churches that was to be distributed among the poor Jews in Jerusalem. Paul brought the offering to Jerusalem in hopes that the outpouring of Gentile generosity would soften the hearts of Jerusalem's Jewish leaders. While there, as an additional gesture of good will, Paul showed his respect for Judaism by using some of his own money to assist some Jewish men in fulfilling a vow they had made.

Even as he worked so hard to bring about reconciliation, however, the Jewish authorities wrongly accused Paul of breaking the law and created such a riot that Paul had to be arrested for his own safekeeping. Later, they brought charges designed to keep the apostle in prison. Paul was moved from Jerusalem to Caesarea, and later transported to Rome. It was probably while there in the dungeons of Rome that Paul wrote the letter that is addressed to the Ephesians in our Bibles, but was probably intended for all the churches. In this letter, Paul first uses the word *ekklesía* in the sense of the church universal.

And this is what Paul says,

> *This is the reason that I Paul am a prisoner for Christ Jesus for the sake of you Gentiles—for surely you have already heard of the commission of God's grace that was given me for you, and how the mystery was made known to me by revelation, as I wrote above in a few words, a reading of which will enable you to perceive my understanding of the mystery of Christ. In former generations this mystery was not made known to humankind, as it has now been revealed to his holy apostles and prophets by the Spirit: that is, the Gentiles have become fellow heirs, members of the same body, and sharers in the promise in Christ Jesus through the gospel.*
>
> *Of this gospel I have become a servant according to the gift of God's grace that was given me by the working of his power. Although I am the very least of all the saints, this grace was given to me to bring to the Gentiles the news of the boundless riches of Christ, and to make everyone see what is the plan of the mystery hidden for ages in God who created all things; so that through the church the wisdom of God in its rich variety might now be made known to the rulers and authorities in the heavenly places. This was in accordance with the eternal pur-*

pose that he has carried out in Christ Jesus our Lord, in whom
we have access to God in boldness and confidence through faith
in him. I pray therefore that you may not lose heart over my
sufferings for you; they are your glory. (Eph 3:1-13)

This was Paul's message—the mystery of the ages—that God's universal plan was to put this fractured world back together again by including *everyone* in the kingdom who wants to belong. That was the secret. That was the good news. You're included. I'm included. Everyone's included. God's love extends to all people.

Now, here is the second part of Paul's message in the text we just read: God has called the *church* to make this truth known throughout the earth. The truth of God is rich and manifold and beyond any of us when it comes to understanding all of it, but *this* we can understand— God's love through Christ Jesus is intended for all persons; we are *all* included. We all can come boldly to God, confident that his grace and his love are sufficient for our present and our future.

God's Mystery for Today

This word of God through Paul is still good news today, and it is still a challenge as well. Here is the good news: *you* are included. Today it's not as hard to convince the church that others should be included as it is to convince many people that God really does love them and that they really are included in his plan.

You may think, "I can't be included because I've committed too many sins."

You may think, "I can't be included because I don't have enough faith."

You may think, "I can't be included because I don't know enough about the Bible."

You may think, "I can't be included because I still have bad habits."

You may think, "I can't be included because I have too many doubts."

Here is the good news: *you're included,* if you want to be. God's love is for you, *whoever* you are, *wherever* you are, *whatever* you have done. God wants to love you and make you a part of his eternal family.

And here's the challenge: God is still relying on the church to make his plan known to the world, to declare the good news to everyone, to become the great inviters who seek out the Scrunges of this world and let them know that the great mystery of the ages has been revealed, and it is this: God's love and God's offer of redemption are universal, and whosoever believes in him shall not perish, but have everlasting life.

CLOUD FIGHTS

Ephesians 6:10-17

The Kingdom of Cloud

There once was a man in the kingdom of Cloud who went out one day to fight.

I say he was a man, and that is almost true, for he was becoming a man, and his purpose that day was to face the test of manhood.

And I speak of the country of Cloud as if it were a true kingdom, and certainly its subjects regarded it as the greatest of all kingdoms, for they had the wisest king in the known lands. But for all that, the kingdom of Cloud was so small that the whole of it rested in a tiny valley between two towering peaks of a massive mountain. The craggy peaks were so tall that they often pierced the clouds, which should tell all you need to know about how the mountain—and the kingdom—got its name.

And I said he went out to fight, but it is not as if he were looking for a fight. In truth, he went out to survive, but he knew he would have to fight to do it.

The kingdom of Cloud was not famous for the strength of its army, though its soldiers were brave and skilled; or for the snowy wool of its sheep, though it was renowned; or even for the cold, clear water that flowed from its one small river, though you would never taste any better. Rather, the tiny land was famous for its goodness. Through all the surrounding lands, people looked at the peaks of Cloud Mountain, and they took note of the hidden valley kingdom, and they repeated the common wisdom: "The kingdom of Cloud is the heart of goodness, and its king is the wisest of all."

There was truth of a fashion in the old adage, for the high king over Cloud was indeed wise, and the one law of his kingdom was that all of his subjects should base their behavior on love for one another. For the most part, the people of Cloud happily followed this one law, and good will filled the land like a mountain mist.

But the king was also wise enough to know that evil men would have no love for his country, and that his subjects must always be prepared to defend themselves from wickedness.

So it was that young Mick, son of Dunam, came to take his test of manhood. The king had decreed that no man could remain in Cloud past his twentieth year unless he had first made a pilgrimage down the mountain and through the lowlands. This may sound backwards to you, for in some other lands young men and women must endure hardship and travel to some holy mountain in order to prove themselves, but those who lived in the kingdom of Cloud were already in a holy place. Their challenge was to leave the safe confines of the highlands and confront the wickedness below.

"This is our refuge," the king would say, "this is our home . . . but the world is bigger than we are, and evil is never satisfied to leave goodness alone. You must learn to recognize the presence of wickedness and the power of evil. You must learn to defend yourself against the wiles of the world."

The would-be men of Cloud were not sent out defenseless, of course. And so when young Mick prepared to make his departure, he came first to the palace armory, for all pilgrims who left the mountain wore the livery of the kingdom of Cloud.

THE ARMOR OF CLOUD

Mick was amazed when he entered the hall and came face to face with Sir Endusan, the captain of the guard. Sir Endusan was a head shorter than Mick, and thin as a rail, but he bore the look of many battles in his wizened face. "So you've come," he said in a distinctive brogue that betrayed the distant land of his birth. "Come to take up your armor. Come to see the world. Come to pit your goodness against the wicked world. Good for you!"

And with that, Sir Endusan sized Mick up with a practiced eye, and from a nail on the wall he took down a wide leather belt and held it out for approval.

Mick looked at this plain, rugged belt, and compared it to the stylish one he was wearing. "But I already have a belt," he said, "and it's much nicer. My mother gave it to me. Can't I keep it on?"

"Young man," answered the captain, "this is a special belt, and there is magic to it. As long as you wear this belt, you will have power to discern between what is real and what is unreal, what is true and what is false. The road you will travel is deceptive. The people you meet may not be what they seem. Wear this belt, and you can see the truth. What is more, as long as you wear this belt, you can only speak the truth. You must take it off if you wish to lie."

So Mick wrapped the wide belt firmly around his waist, and he did indeed feel that he stood more upright, that he could see more clearly. No sooner had he done this than Sir Endusan almost knocked him over with something that looked like a giant silver turtle shell with straps. "Hold this on your chest," he said, and he proceeded to buckle the straps and to draw them tight.

"I'm not sure I like this," Mick gasped, as Sir Endusan pulled the straps tight. "Won't this thing restrict me? Won't it keep me from moving freely?"

"Aye!" said the captain. "This chest protector will keep your heart from making bad decisions. It will force you to keep your appetites under control and your desires in check. You'll need that, for there are many who will tempt you. The old soldiers have a saying: 'Keep your chestplate strapped on tight; your heart will lead you to the right.' And I have a saying: 'You can't go wrong if you leave it on!'"

Mick wasn't so sure. He was still trying to shift the breastplate into a more comfortable position when Endusan asked, "And what size shoes do you wear?"

"Shoes?" Mick shouted. *"Shoes?* I'm wearing my best hiking boots now! I bought them just for this trip!"

"Oh, but those are too big and bulky," said Sir Endusan. "They will slow you down, they will hurt your feet. They will be bad news before the journey is over." And he handed up a simple pair of high-top running shoes with clouds stitched onto the sides.

"These are enchanted shoes," he said. "They will show you the way to peace, and they will take you to places you need to go. Many people there are in the lowlands, people who need to hear the words that you must tell them. They need to know how we live here in the kingdom of Cloud. As long as you wear these shoes, you'll know what to say that is good and helpful. You cannot curse anyone, or demean anyone, or say a harmful word unless you take them off."

And so young Mick took off his heavy boots and put on his new cloud shoes, and he did feel that he walked easier, that he was more in touch with the earth, that he had a clearer sense of direction.

"These feel nice," Mick said, "Now I'm ready to go!"

"Oh no, you're not!" said the captain. "But you're halfway there. Now, you're right-handed? Good! Hold your left arm across your chest like this." He began to fiddle with something Mick could not see. The young man briefly felt something press down on his arm, but when Sir Endusan stepped away with a nod of approval, Mick could not tell any difference at all.

"What is this?" Mick cried. "A make-believe shield?"

The old captain smiled the smile of one who has explained this many times, and he said, "Master Mick, you are correct that this is your shield—and you are not mistaken in thinking that it is invisible.

"That's the trick of it! You cannot see it, and most of the time, you cannot feel it. The wearing of the shield is a test of your faith, you see. You must hold on to your shield, even when you cannot see it, even when you cannot feel it. When you go into the world, your greatest battle will not be with other men whom you can see, but with dark powers that may be hidden from your eyes. The black demons will be all over you from the moment you leave our kingdom's gates, but they can see what you cannot see. They can see your shield of faith, and they know that they cannot penetrate it, and so they will leave you alone. But, because they cannot touch you, you may question if they are really there.

"And so be warned, young Mick." Endusan was holding him by the shoulders now, and looking him straight in the eyes. "If you ever decide that you no longer need this shield, at the moment you cast it aside, the demons of doubt will be upon you, and all their cohorts with them. Hold it tight!"

With those words the old captain was near tears. "Hold on tight though you see it not, and your faith will see you through!"

When Sir Endusan turned him loose and turned away, Mick realized that he had been holding his breath. He let it out slowly, and took several deep breaths while the old soldier rustled through another pile of gear. He came back with a gleaming helmet of shining brass with clouds of silver on either side. "This is your helmet," he said, "Kneel here so I can put it on you."

Mick felt foolish kneeling, but he obeyed, and the captain put the helmet on his head with a great seriousness that bordered on ceremony. "The helmet of a soldier of Cloud is the symbol of his citizenship and a testimony of his allegiance. It will protect your mind and direct your thinking. Wear it with pride and honor as a citizen of the kingdom of Cloud."

"But this helmet is really heavy!" said Mick. "Do you mean I have to wear this thing all the way down the mountain?"

"Oh, yes," replied Endusan, with some weariness, "and all the way back up, too—assuming, of course, that you make it back. You could just throw it away and live the rest of your life in the lowlands, my boy, and there are some who do—but you would no longer be a citizen of Cloud. Your ears would be unprotected, and your mind would quickly be lost to the voices of the world below, and you would never find your way back. If you keep this helmet on, it will help you remember who you are, and it will become your salvation."

"Then I shall wear it," replied the young man, "though my neck grows tired and my ears grow itchy, I will wear it. I am proud to be a citizen of Cloud, and I will not lose myself to wicked ways."

Sir Endusan held Mick in a somber gaze for a long moment, and said only, "Let us hope you remain sure of yourself, and true to your word. Now, there is one more thing I must give you."

The captain drew from his own scabbard a shining sword and held it out in reverent hands. "Young Mick," he said with a solemn voice, "the blessing of the king himself is upon this sword, and the words of the one law of love are engraved on its blade. This sword is not what it appears. It is not an instrument of death, but of life. Your other armaments will provide all the defensive protection you need. This sword is the only offensive weapon you have, but you may use it only for good, and not for evil. It is a sword of light.

"When some dark knight of temptation comes against you, your helmet will protect your mind, your shield and your breastplate will protect your heart. There is no promise that you will never be hurt, and no assurance that you can protect those you love. But as long as you hold to this sword, to the word of the king, to the law of love, you will not only endure, but you will show others the way out of darkness and into the light. Yes, Mick, you may bring others back with you to the kingdom of Cloud, for this is a special kingdom, and though it looks small to the world, there is always room for more, and it will never be crowded. The king has made it so. How do you think I got here, lad?

"Now, my young friend, you may go. Go forth from the gates and into the world, but never forget that the goodness of Cloud and the power of the king go with you. Always keep your armor close, and the dark powers cannot harm you. Always keep your sword in your hand and its words on your lips, and others will follow you home. Go now, with the love of this old captain, and with the blessing of your king."

There was a heavy moment of silence, broken finally by the sound of Mick's new shoes squeaking on the floor as he made an about-face, held himself as tall as he could, and ventured forth into the world. As the sound of Mick's footsteps echoed and died in the hallway, Sir Endusan knelt in the midst of his armory, and he prayed with all his heart that Mick would keep his armor on.

Finally, be strong in the Lord and in the strength of his power.
Put on the whole armor of God, so that you may be able to
stand against the wiles of the devil. For our struggle is not
against enemies of blood and flesh, but against the rulers,

against the authorities, against the cosmic powers of this present darkness, against the spiritual forces of evil in the heavenly places.

Therefore take up the whole armor of God, so that you may be able to withstand on that evil day, and having done everything, to stand firm.

Stand therefore, and fasten the belt of truth around your waist, and put on the breastplate of righteousness. As shoes for your feet put on whatever will make you ready to proclaim the gospel of peace. With all of these, take the shield of faith, with which you will be able to quench all the flaming arrows of the evil one. Take the helmet of salvation, and the sword of the Spirit, which is the word of God. (Eph 6:10-17)

Author's note: *Just for fun, the names in this story reflect significant words in the text. Mick is the "son of Dunam." Forms of the Greek verb* dunamai, *which means "to be strong" or "to be able," are found in v. 10 and v. 11. Endusan, the armorer's name, is taken from the verb* enduo, *which appears in v. 11 as the aorist imperative* endusasthe, *and means "to put on." Mick's name calls to mind the word for "sword,"* machaira, *which appears in v. 17 with reference to the "sword of the Spirit."*

Part 3:
UNEXPECTED VOICES

MOON-REACHING

Exodus 19:1-6

JUST BE-CLAWS

High on a rugged spur of a desolate mountain, deep in the Sinai desert, there lived a young golden eagle with the beak of a champion and the heart of a chicken. His father bore the family name "Nesher," which is Hebrew for "eagle," and his mother's name was "Canaphim" (ku-nah-PHEEM), which means "wings." I'm sure you understand that all of the eagles in that part of the world speak Hebrew.

After the eaglet was hatched in that high mountain aerie, he quickly developed a unique personality, but not the kind that wins admiration in the society of eagles. The young eagle was afraid of heights, and he tended to hold on so tightly to the woven brush making up his nest that he quickly picked up the nickname "Teffrey," which is short for "Tepherim," which we would translate as "claws."

As young Claws began to grow toward maturity, his parents persistently pushed him toward the edge of the nest, because that is what good eagle parents do. Yet, every time Claws peered over the rim to look down at the valley floor several thousand feet below, he got the same quiver in his stomach he had felt the first time his mother brought him the chewed-up remains of a desert mouse for supper. He kept hoping he would learn to like heights as much as he had grown to love mice, but it was a slow process.

Claws knew, of course, that one day he would have to leap from the edge of that nest and learn to fly and hunt for himself. His sister had moved out of the nest days ago. He intended, however, to put it off as long as he could.

Time passed and Claws showed no curiosity or desire to fly. Ultimately, however, his mother Canaphim decided to take matters into her own wings. She sensed an opportunity on a day when her sharp eyes spotted movement on the lower slopes of the mountain. It was a single man, bringing a flock of sheep to pasture on the tender grass that appeared for a brief time each year.

Claws had never seen a sheep, much less a man, so when his mother called he momentarily dropped his defenses and crept up to look over the edge and test his own eagle eyes. He was just thinking of how those sheep looked remarkably like little white ants when he felt a gentle but forceful push from behind. Before he had time to clamp down with his vise-like talons, the young eagle found himself falling over the edge of the nest and hurtling toward the valley floor.

Now, let's give him some credit. Claws *tried* to fly. He flapped his wings a few times, though not necessarily at the same time, and he could not gain any purchase on the air. Claws, of course, was horrified. Kicking his feet more than his wings, he soon resigned himself to a quick death on the rocks below.

As the terrified eagle tumbled downward, the features of the valley floor began to expand: trees, rocks, and even the sheep grew larger and larger. As he fell closer and closer to the earth, Claws could even see the astonished look on that lonely shepherd's upturned face—but then suddenly, he felt an unexpected movement beneath his frantic feet. The mother eagle had circled overhead to watch her son's descent. When it became evident that he would not make it on his own, she stooped and dove. With extraordinary speed and accuracy born of hunting swift desert rodents, she swooped beneath the frightened eaglet and caught him on her powerful back.

As Claws dug in with all his might, she absorbed the shock with outstretched wings and went into a shallow glide right over the startled sheep. With practiced ease, she began to move her wings, beating the air in long, sweeping strokes, gradually gaining altitude in a slow, graceful, circling climb back toward the nest.

When Claws finally reopened his eyes, he looked from right to left and back again, watching his mother's wings at work in midair. *Oh,* he thought, *so that's how it's done.* He tentatively spread his own wings a bit and felt the rush of air lift him slightly from his piggy-back perch. Claws found his fear being transformed into exhilaration.

Sensing that her son was ready for another try, Canaphim went into a gradual dive. The onrushing air swept Claws free and immediately his wings went into action, but slower and more steadily than before. One, two, three beats, and he found himself gaining altitude, then gliding smoothly downward, then climbing again with long, powerful, heart-throbbing strokes.

Down below, the solitary shepherd stared in open-mouthed fascination. He was unable to let the moment pass in silence, so he let out a hoarse cheer for the young eagle. Then he began talking to himself, as lonesome shepherds are prone to do. "Well, Moses," he muttered, "there's something you never saw in Egypt."

And he thought perhaps it was the most marvelous thing he would ever see, until he looked back up at the mountainside and beheld a burning bush.

JUST BECAUSE

No one knows just how long it took, but there came a day when Moses returned to that mountain. This time he was not leading a small flock of sheep, but a huge and noisy multitude of men and women. God had spoken to Moses the last time he was here, and had promised to bring him safely back after delivering the children of Israel from their captivity in Egypt. You know that story. Now here they were. Moses was leading and the people were complaining.

Moses was hoping that God would speak to him again, and he was not disappointed:

> *In the third month of the exodus of the children of Israel from*
> *the land of Egypt,*
> *on the very day they came to the wilderness of Sinai*

> *(they had journeyed from Rephidim and came to the wilderness of Sinai and camped in the wilderness; there Israel camped before the mountain)—*
> *Moses went up to God,*
> *and Yahweh called to him from the mountain, saying*
> *"Thus shall you say to the family of Jacob, and declare to the children of Israel:*
> *'You yourselves have seen what I did to the Egyptians,*
> *and how I lifted you up on wings of eagles, and I brought you to myself.*
> *And now, if you will pay careful attention to my voice, and will keep my covenant,*
> *you will be to me a special treasure among all the peoples—for all the earth is mine—*
> *and you will be to me a kingdom of priests, and a holy nation.'*
> *These are the words which you will speak to the children of Israel." (Exod 19:1-6, author's translation)*

This is one of the most powerful texts in all of the Old Testament. It begins with a stirring call to remember God's work. It offers to us a framework for response to God's grace. And it gives to believers a special role within God's kingdom. It is God's way of saying, "You are special. Let's work together."

<u>A Call to Remember (v. 4)</u>

> *"You yourselves have seen what I did to the Egyptians, and how I lifted you up on wings of eagles, and I brought you to myself."*

We all need reminding, every now and then, of what God has done for us. With their own eyes, the Hebrews had seen the plagues strike Egypt. They had seen the waters roll back so they could cross the sea that led to freedom, and then watched the same waters close in and crush the pursuing Egyptians.

But God did not stop with deliverance. As the people marched through the wilderness, God hovered over them like a mother eagle. The people offered little in the way of cooperation and much in the way of complaints, but God provided water, food, and rest. God carried them when they could not carry themselves.

So it was that Moses later used this same image to remind Israel of the Lord's care. "Like an eagle that stirs up its nest, that hovers over its young, he spread his wings and caught them, he carried them on his pinions" (Deut 32:11-12). God had brought them to Sinai for a purpose. God wanted Israel to learn how to fly and had brought them here to teach them. They had come a long way but had a long way to go.

We have traveled a different path than Israel, but God has also delivered us and sustained us. Wherever we are and however we got here, we may also be confronted by God's presence and challenged by God's call. We have come a long way, but have a long way to go.

A Framework for Response (v. 5a)

"And now, if you will pay careful attention to my voice, and will keep my covenant . . ."

When our English Bibles read "obey my voice," what they are translating is a special Hebrew construction that combines two forms of the same verb for emphasis. Literally, it means "if you will hearingly hear," or "if listening, you will listen." To truly hear God's voice is to obey God's command. This passage is the preface to the Ten Commandments. God was offering to Israel a covenant based on his grace and his gift of relationship, but there was also a part for Israel to play.

In our time, God continues to offer us the opportunity of a covenant relationship, not just through words carved in stone, but through the Word made flesh, through Jesus Christ. As with Israel, though, our participation in God's covenant family begins with acceptance and continues with obedience.

Such obedience is best expressed through faith and loyalty. As Yahweh called upon Israel to live in obedience, so Jesus said to his followers, "If you love me, keep my commandments" (John 14:15). In all three Synoptic Gospels, Jesus makes it clear that his commandments are to love God and to love others with the same kind of unselfish love he demonstrated toward us.

A Special Identity (vv. 5b-6a)

When we respond through faith and obedience, God gives to us a special identity: "... you will be to me a special treasure among all the peoples—for all the earth is mine—and you will be to me a kingdom of priests, and a holy nation."

God has promised to make us his *special treasure* among all the peoples of the earth. This translates a specialized Hebrew word. An ancient Near Eastern king could look out over his realm and say, "All this land is mine, these people are mine, all the harvest is mine." And there is a sense in which it would be true. But if he took out a sword his father had given him, or a ring from his wife, or looked at the face of his newborn child, he would say, "This is my *segullah*, my special treasure." That is what we become to God: a special treasure.

God also says we are to become a *kingdom of priests* and *a holy nation*. This is perhaps the deepest root of the Baptist doctrine that we call the priesthood of the believer. We believe that every believer may pray directly without calling upon a professional priest, and that every believer has the right and the responsibility of reading the Scripture for himself or herself. It means all of us must seek, with the guidance of the community of faith and the leadership of the Holy Spirit, to determine God's will for ourselves.

As a kingdom of priests, we also have responsibilities to others. We are to serve as the mediators of God's message to a world that is lost. We intercede for others in our prayers. *That is, we represent others before God, and we represent God to others.*

When we take this relationship and responsibility seriously, we will truly be a holy nation. This does not refer to purity alone, but to our distinctiveness. In the Old Testament, the word "holy" means "set apart." We are God's "set-apart people," called to do God's work.

This great Old Testament promise was so memorable that Peter called upon it in his own charge to New Testament believers when he said, "But you are a chosen race, a royal priesthood, a holy nation,

God's own people, that you may proclaim the mighty acts of him who called you out of darkness into his marvelous light. Once you were not a people, but now you are God's people" (1 Pet 2:9-10a).

WHERE TO?

God wanted the people of Israel to rise above the world's allure and learn to fly, and God wants the same for those who bear Christ's name today.

Now, truly trusting in God is a bit like stepping off a cliff and believing God will catch us. To follow Christ, we must step from the security of our cultural nest, believing that God has a better life in store for us.

How sad it is to think of an eagle that never leaves the nest and never achieves the joy of flight or the potential God has placed within it. And how sad to think of a person who never leaves the security of the familiar to discover the abundant life God has in store for those who will receive it.

It is equally grievous to imagine a church that idolizes the security of its nest. It is the church that serves as our flight training school. It is the community of faith that gives us opportunities to stretch our wings and soar to new spiritual heights. It is our spiritual family that should challenge us if we start getting lazy and spend our time circling on the wind. It is the people of God who recognize our giftedness and encourage our participation in doing God's work. The church is not just a hangar where we go to retreat; it is a flight deck that sends us on mission. To the extent we prove ourselves obedient and willing to follow God's way, we can fly. And even if we should run into sudden storms or microbursts or wind shear, God is still with us and will aid us.

We remember the unforgettable words of Isaiah: "But those who wait for the Lord shall renew their strength, they shall mount up with wings like eagles, they shall run and not be weary, they shall walk and not faint" (Isa 40:31).

When our son Samuel was a toddler, there was a night when the moon was full, and the two of us were out in the cul-de-sac, just sort of hanging out. The moon was high over a neighbor's house, framed by several trees, huge and bright and fringed with faint clouds. I showed the moon to Samuel, and a big grin came over his face. "Moon!" he said. Then, reaching up with his arms, he jumped into the air again and again, saying, "Reach! Reach!" It was a special thing to see the wide-eyed innocence of a little child who thinks he can reach the moon.

Do we ever feel just idealistic enough and childlike enough to think we can shoot for the moon, and make it? When we put our trust in the Lord and follow God's way, the moon is just the beginning of the places we can go.

A BETTER BUNNY

Jeremiah 31:31-34

BILLY BOB'S CHANGE OF HEART

Billy Bob Bunny was the most rascally rabbit in the Piney Woods, and everybody knew it, including his mother. She thought it might be because he was such a small bunny, except for his ears, which were too big for his body. Billy Bob was too little to be a bully, but that didn't stop the hyper hare from being a pest who often stuck his whiskers into places they didn't belong.

The pesky bunny pulled so many tricks on his cousin Jackie Rabbit that Jackie wouldn't play with him anymore. He was sort of sweet on his classmate Betsy Beaver, but one day he made fun of her big buck teeth and she broadsided him with her big flat tail. *Honestly!* thought Billy Bob. *Just because I said she could eat corn on the cob from the opposite side of a picket fence is no reason for violence!* Some lessons were hard for him to learn.

Billy Bob tried to make friends with some of the big kids at school. Baxter Bear seemed to enjoy the bunny's company for a while, but when Billy Bob started cracking fat jokes and called Baxter a lardbucket, he swatted him with a big forepaw and sent him tumbling head over hind feet down the hill. When he finally stopped rolling, Billy Bob picked himself up and shook his fur and scratched behind his ears with a thumping sound. He wasn't hurt except for his pride, but he decided not to return to school that day, and hopped off in search of further excitement.

Soon Billy Bob came to the big hollow tree where old Mr. Porcupine ran the "Piney Woods General Store and Soda Shoppe." Since he was thirsty, Billy Bob hopped in for a drink of carrot juice.

Now, Mr. Porcupine was just about every young critter's favorite adult. Cubs and kids and kits and pups loved to visit his store because he would listen to their stories while he made berry shakes, and he remembered their names and their birthdays.

The store was empty when Mr. Porcupine heard the little bell ring as Billy Bob brushed against the last limb leading into the store. The storekeeper's bristles had already turned gray on the ends, and he'd seen a lot of brash young bunnies hop through. He knew that Billy Bob was supposed to be in school, but he held his peace because it was obvious that the little rascal was running from something.

Mr. Porcupine poured Billy Bob a nice tall glass of fresh carrot juice, and he wasn't even surprised when the little upstart gulped it down and licked his whiskers and said he didn't have any money to pay for it. Mr. Porcupine scratched his chin and suggested that maybe Billy Bob would like to do some work around the store to pay for his juice.

The young bunny immediately accepted. He was a bit surprised that the most respected animal in the woods apparently wanted to be his friend. So Billy Bob put on a little white apron and started sweeping. He even worked hard for half an hour or so. Was Billy Bob becoming a better bunny?

After school that day, several of the kids from school stopped in for an afternoon snack. Mr. Porcupine had gone up to the branch bank to make a deposit, and left Billy Bob alone to tend the soda fountain. Billy Bob seemed to have found his niche. He fixed Baxter Bear a honey shake and peeled some fresh birch bark for Betsy Beaver. Jackie Rabbit ordered carrot sticks, but Billy Bob had eaten them all, so Jackie had to settle for alfalfa sprouts.

The other kids were quite impressed that Billy Bob was working for Mr. Porcupine, and the smug young bunny saw this as a golden opportunity to show off for his classmates. Unfortunately, the scamp had never learned to boast about himself without making fun of someone else. When they asked him how he got the job, Billy Bob said, "Aw, it was easy! Old Porky doesn't really know how to run this store, and he recognized that a bright young bunny like me could really turn things around for him. Yes sir, I've got old Needle Nose wrapped around my cottontail."

Billy Bob was on a roll. "Mr. P's nothing but an overgrown pincushion anyway. With all those porcupine spines, he's got no room for brains! Old Quillface lets me do anything I want!"

Then, as if to prove it, when Billy Bob took the money for the honey shake and the birch bark and the alfalfa sprouts, he put it in his own pocket instead of the knothole Mr. Porcupine had showed him. Then he poured another glass of carrot juice for himself, hopped up on the counter, and said, "Yep, when I get through showing old Bristle Britches the ropes, you won't even recognize the place!"

Billy Bob was enjoying himself so much that it took him some moments to realize that his classmates had become very quiet, and were nervously nibbling their snacks while their eyes darted around behind Billy Bob and then back at each other.

When the little rabbit with the big mouth turned to see what they were looking at, his heart fell down into his bunny belly and he suddenly felt very sick. There was Mr. Porcupine, and *he had heard the whole thing!*

Billy Bob's ears stood straight up and he hopped clean over the soda fountain and took off into the woods with tears in his eyes and fright in his heart. "Oh, why did I do that?" he said aloud to himself. "Why can't I keep my big mouth shut?" Then Billy Bob remembered the money he had taken and he cried even more. "Mr. Porcupine will kill me! He'll hold me down and sit on me with his porcupine spines and I'll look like a carrot strainer. Oh, why can't I be good? I'll never get another chance now!" With that, the frightened bunny crawled into a hollow log that was one of his favorite hiding places, and he sobbed big bunny tears until the fur on his face was soaking wet.

The other children looked for Billy Bob so they could make fun of the foolish bunny, but they couldn't find him, and they didn't look long. Billy Bob stayed in the old log for a long time. He didn't come home for supper, and when it began to grow dark, the lonely blubbering bunny became very frightened. He thought he would die for sure when he heard the loud "Hoo! Hoo!" of a hoot owl, but then he heard another sound. It was a voice—a familiar voice, an old, scratchy voice—and it was shouting, "Billy Bob! Billy Bob!"

The voice, of course, belonged to Mr. Porcupine, and Billy Bob knew it. *Oh no!* he thought. *Now I'm gonna get it! I can't let him find me!* And with that he scrambled further up into the hollow log. Billy Bob had never learned to do anything quietly, and the sharp-eared Mr. Porcupine heard the bunny's claws scratching against the wood. He remembered hiding in hollow logs when he was a scared and lonely youngster, so he put two and two together and peeked into the log.

"Billy Bob!" he said. "Come on out of there!"

"But I can't!" the bunny bawled in a whiny voice. "I'm in too much trouble!"

"Well," said Mr. Porcupine, "I don't deny that you've done plenty to get yourself into trouble! But I've had my eye on you, Billy Bob. I've seen you play tricks and call names just to get attention. I know it's not easy being the littlest bunny in the woods. Now I expect an apology from you for the names you called me. And I expect you to return the money you took. But I don't want to hurt you, Billy Bob. I want to be your friend. So, what do you say, little bunny—would you like to come out and start all over? I'll forgive you for what you said. I'll even promise to forget those bad things you did. What about it, Billy Bob—would you like to be friends again?"

The little bunny couldn't believe what his oversized ears were hearing, and his nose twitched so much that he could hardly answer, but he cried out, "Yes!" in a squeaky voice and came scrambling out of the log and hid his face in Mr. Porcupine's soft belly.

From that day on, Billy Bob was on his way to becoming a better bunny. Mr. Porcupine's example of love and grace began to change Billy Bob, *from the heartside out.*

A HARD-HEARTED PEOPLE

Many years ago, a little country named Israel with oversized ambitions and too much pride had the opportunity to become the special friends of Almighty God. But, despite God's friendship, so the Bible says, they rebelled against him and chose to follow their own way. They tried to do better, sometimes, but they always seemed to trip over their own big feet.

In time, they found themselves stuffed into the hollow log of exile in a foreign land. The northern kingdom of Israel was conquered by the Assyrians in 722 BC, and the southern kingdom of Judah was overrun by the Babylonians in 587 BC. Both enemy nations took many prisoners from the leading families of Israel and forced them to leave their homes and live in prison camps in Mesopotamia.

It was a horrible, scary time—a long, dark night in a foreign land—but as with many bad things, something good came out of it. The people's sad experience in Babylon had caused them to take a hard look at their lives, and some of them began to see how they had turned away from the God who befriended them. They saw how many mistakes they had made. They began to pray that the God who once had befriended them would come and find them in their darkness, would forgive their failures, and would grant them another chance.

A Big-hearted God

The old prophet Jeremiah had tried his best to keep the people of Israel from going into exile to begin with. He had often pointed to their twisted hearts and reminded them of the grave danger of following their own hearts' desires instead of walking after God's heart. On one occasion he said,

> *O Jerusalem, wash your heart clean of wickedness so that you*
> *may be saved.*
> *How long shall your evil schemes lodge within you?*
> *For a voice declares from Dan, and proclaims disaster from*
> *Mount Ephraim.*
> *Tell the nations, "Here they are!"*
> *Proclaim against Jerusalem,*
> *"Besiegers come from a distant land;*
> *they shout against the cities of Judah.*
> *They have closed in around her like watchers of a field,*

because she has rebelled against me, says the Lord.
Your ways and your doings have brought this upon you.
This is your doom; how bitter it is! It has reached your very
heart." (Jer 4:14-18)

On another day, Jeremiah cried out,

But this people has a stubborn and rebellious heart; they have
turned aside and gone away.
They do not say in their hearts,
"Let us fear the Lord our God, who gives the rain in its season,
the autumn rain and the spring rain,
and keeps for us the weeks appointed for the harvest."
Your iniquities have turned these away, and your sins have
deprived you of good. (Jer 5:23-25)

Jeremiah argued that Israel had serious heart trouble. He urged the people to wash their hearts clean of wickedness (4:14), and even to "circumcise their hearts" as a sign of devotion to God (4:4). But the people of Israel were stubborn. They refused to change, and their sins caught up with them.

Once they found themselves lost and alone, deep in the darkness of exile, many thoughtful Israelites began to reconsider. They wept in repentance. They called upon the Lord for help. They appointed their theologians to find a solution. But they feared it was too late.

So, you can imagine how happy the people were to hear Jeremiah offer a different kind of message, a prophecy of hope and consolation:

The days are surely coming, says the Lord, when I will make a
new covenant with the house of Israel and the house of Judah.
*   It will not be like the covenant that I made with their*
ancestors when I took them by the hand to bring them out of
the land of Egypt—a covenant that they broke, though I was
their husband, says the Lord.
*   But this is the covenant that I will make with the house of*
Israel after those days, says the Lord: I will put my law within
them, and I will write it on their hearts; and I will be their
God, and they shall be my people.

No longer shall they teach one another, or say to each other, "Know the Lord," for they shall all know me, from the least of them to the greatest, says the Lord; for I will forgive their iniquity, and remember their sin no more. (Jer 31:31-34).

Here is gospel. Here is grace. Here is God's second chance to a people who have blown their chance too many times already. The passage promises a new covenant for a new life. It seemed too good to be true, and it didn't happen immediately. The people who first heard the message did not live to see its ultimate fulfillment, but Christians who look backward in time came to believe that God's promise came true in the life and work of Jesus Christ.

Jeremiah saw a coming day when people could have an entirely new kind of relationship with God in which the old, conditional covenant would be replaced by something new. Israel had come to regard the law of God and the rituals of temple worship as something entirely separate from daily life. The law was something *external*, written on stone tablets, taught by the priests, argued in the city gates, and exercised in the court.

But something new was going to happen. God promised to bring about a new covenant relationship in which his law would no longer be written on stone or in scrolls alone, but would be written on human hearts: "I will put my law within them, and I will write it on their hearts; and I will be their God, and they shall be my people."

Sometimes people want to demonstrate the permanence of their love by getting a tattoo of a heart or some other object, perhaps with the name of their loved one written across it. Jeremiah said God's law would be written upon our hearts. That is what happens when God's presence is also living and working within us through the love of Jesus. He writes his law on our hearts like an internal tattoo—a mark that is written in blood, but not our own.

We teach our children that God lives in their hearts, and they believe it. I remember one evening when our daughter Bethany was four years old, and we asked her to say the blessing before dinner. Bethany's blessings rarely had anything to do with food. As she prayed, she said, "Thank you God for being in my heart. Don't go away now! Back and forth, back and forth . . . ." My wife Jan peeked, and saw that Bethany was rocking back and forth in the chair, giggling. She was checking to see if God could keep up with her when she rocked back and forth, that he didn't leave her heart when she moved.

God wants youth and adults to believe that he lives in our hearts as well. We may not think as concretely as a small child who wonders whether God can keep up with us. We may think more abstractly about God's presence, but we cannot fully understand it any more than a child does. There is something very mystical about the way God lives and works within us. We don't have to fully understand it in order to believe it.

We know that God truly lives in us when we see a change in our attitudes. We develop an internal sense of what is right and wrong. We develop a new compassion that leads us to react to harm with forgiveness and to be proactive in showing tangible love toward others. God's law is written on our hearts when God's Spirit indwells our hearts.

Jesus told his disciples that he was giving to them a new law to replace the old one, and this is it: "Love one another, as I have loved you." That is the law of love. It means nothing when it is written in a book, but it means everything when it is written on our hearts. The decisions we make, the actions we take, are not determined by a book full of rules but by a heart full of God.

When we come to understand Christ's love, and to experience his care, it changes our lives—from the heartside out. Jeremiah looked to a day when God would say, "I will forgive their iniquity, and remember their sins no more." That is what happens when we trust in Christ. We are forgiven. Our slate is wiped clean. The grace of God purifies our past and sets us on a new road with a new heart.

In the love of Christ, we all can learn to become better bunnies, because the law of love is written on our hearts in the person of Christ, whose Spirit lives in our hearts and lives.

We don't have to feel lost and alone, stuck in a hollow log that is leading nowhere, longing for someone to set us free. There is someone waiting for us, looking for us, calling our names. Are we ready to come out?

DEEP WATER
Luke 5:1-11

A Sermon in a Boat (vv. 1-3)

(Simon Peter's boat speaks slowly in a deep, deadpan, "Forrest Gump" type of voice. How much personality can a wooden fishing boat have?)

It was morning still, but the sun was well up in the sky. It was quiet in the little bay where Simon and Andrew had dragged me out of the water, over the smooth stones of the rocky beach, just far enough to keep me from sliding back into the lake and floating away.

It's not a bad life, being a boat. I get around. I meet interesting people. Sometimes I get to stay out all night and then sleep all day in the sun, and that's fun. It's true that I'm often half-filled with smelly fish, but the boys are always good about washing out the slime after a fishing trip. This morning, though, they had nothing to wash but their nets. We had spent all night on the lake and visited all their favorite fishing holes, but they came up empty. That doesn't happen often, and they cuss when it does.

People eat a lot of fish around here, you know—more than any other meat. There are fishermen on the Mediterranean coast who bring in big saltwater fish, but the main source of freshwater fish is right here in the Sea of Galilee, or Lake Tiberias, or Lake Gennesaret, depending on who's talking. You may know that the lake has three main kinds of fish, but two of those are worthless: big bony carp that nobody wants to eat, and ugly catfish that the Jews won't eat because they don't have proper fins and scales. All the fishermen try to catch a nice hand-sized panfish, a type of tilapia. My boss man Simon became so famous as a fisherman that folks started calling it "St. Peter's fish."

But, as I said, there weren't any of those to be found last night, and so Simon was in a foul mood when we came back to shore. He was grumbling under his breath as he dragged the nets off to wash and mend in the shade. He was quiet while he worked, though. He wasn't one for whistling or exchanging unnecessary pleasantries, even with his brother Andrew or his partners James and John.

I was rocking gently on the little swells that lapped against the shore, and the flies were buzzing about my hull in search of lunch when I first noticed the noise. At first it sounded like more flies, just a big humming in the background. Then the buzz turned into the sounds of people—lots of them—walking and talking at the same time, acting as if they were in a hurry to get somewhere. Soon I saw a big crowd coming around the bend of the path that led down to our little bay, and the rabbi Jesus was at their head. I had seen him before, and I had heard Simon and the boys talking about him. He was some sort of traveling preacher and miracle-worker. They said he had done some amazing things, so I wasn't surprised that he had a big posse behind him.

It looked like everybody in the crowd wanted a piece of Jesus, and he was doing his best to be kind, but it was obvious that they were pressing him hard. He tried to stand on the shore and teach, but they almost pushed him in the water. He looked at me and got an idea. Then he hollered at Simon, and ran across the little beach and jumped right over my starboard side. Simon was right behind him with his nets under one arm, pushing me out into the water and then clambering in behind Jesus. Simon grabbed the oars and pulled us away from shore just far enough to keep anyone else from swimming out to climb on board, and then he went to my stern and cast an anchor from each side.

Jesus sat down right on my prow and faced the crowd. He looked tired, like it was the first time he'd had a chance to sit down in a while. Then he began to teach them. I have been used to haul everything from fish to passengers before, but that was the first time I've ever been used as a pulpit.

A Miracle in the Nets (vv. 4-7)

After saying all he intended to say, Jesus told Simon to pull up the anchors and head out to deep water so he could try fishing again. Simon appeared to be a little flustered. He liked Jesus, of course, but the rabbi was trained as a *carpenter*, of all things. He could probably build a boat better than he could fish in one. What did he know about fish? So Simon complained about it a little. He reminded Jesus that he'd already fished all night for nothing.

Jesus could have been offended, but it didn't seem to bother him. He looked back at Simon and said, "Just do what I tell you and see what happens."

We didn't even have to go that far—we were still in sight and hearing of the crowd on shore when Jesus told Simon to throw out his net, and it started to drag the old cuss down almost before he finished playing it out. I'm only twenty-seven feet long, just under eight feet wide, and about four and a half feet deep, so it doesn't take much to make me unstable.

When Simon pulled on that net I began to list so far to port that I was certain he would turn me over, but together he and Jesus called out for James and John to bring their boat, too. Before we got all those fish on board, they almost capsized both of us. We made it back, but we were both riding low in the water from the heavy load of fish.

A Confession amid the Fish (vv. 8-9)

Simon was a professional, so he was all business until we safely reached the shore, but as soon as we landed, he fell to his knees in front of Jesus, right in the middle of that great pile of fish. I've never seen Simon so moved by anything. He cried out, "Go away from me, Lord, for I am a sinful man!"

Well, that was stating the obvious. Everyone knew Simon was a sinner. Of course, they knew they were sinners, too. None of the men who worked the boats for a living worried too much about keeping kosher and following the law. They were just good old boys who loved to fish and who drank too much on Saturday night.

Simon had seen Jesus do surprising things before, but that net-load of fish seemed to put him over the top. He seemed to think that Jesus was a little too close to God for comfort. He was afraid somebody as sinful as he was would be bound to get zapped pretty quickly if he hung out with somebody that close to the Lord.

But Jesus was pretty cool about it all. He told Simon to get his face out of the fish, and said, "Don't let this scare you . . . before long, you'll be catching people!" That's all he said. He didn't explain what he meant, but trusted Simon to figure it out.

The crowd on shore was obviously hungry, so Simon just motioned them toward the boats, and soon they were swarming over my gunwales and scooping up fish like looters during a riot. And that provided all the diversion Jesus needed to break away from the crowd. I last saw him headed south, but he wasn't alone. Simon was right behind him, and James, and John. Simon left me! His boat! His livelihood! He left his nets. Left the most profitable catch of fish he had ever made. Left us all to follow Jesus. I didn't like it in the least, but people rarely ask boats for their opinion.

A Lesson for Readers

We are grateful to Simon's boat for sharing with us his memories of that memorable day when Jesus challenged Simon and James and John to follow him. The story is so familiar and the truths of the story are so obvious that we are in danger of missing them.

Some things are so obvious that they don't take a lot of interpreting:

(1) Jesus is Lord.
(2) Jesus calls us to follow.
(3) Jesus calls us to go fishing for others.

Through his words and his actions, Jesus made it abundantly clear that he was not just another man—not even a great magician or healer. What he taught and what he did demonstrated his kinship with God the Creator and Sustainer of all. That is why Simon fell on his face in a pile of fish: he realized he was in the presence of God, and that made him particularly aware of his personal failure and unworthiness.

We know what that's like. We know that we are sinners, too. We know that we have failed countless times, even when we've tried to do what is right. We know what it is to fish all night and catch nothing, to work long and hard with little discernible result. The truth is, we know that feeling so well that it has become comfortable for us. It suits us just fine that Simon didn't catch anything. When the power of God goes to work, it scares us silly.

We know that we are not worthy of the Lord's presence, not worthy of the Lord's invitation, not worthy of the Lord's forgiveness, not worthy of claiming the Lord's name in our witness. We are sinners. Something about us smells like fish and won't wash off.

But that doesn't matter to Jesus. He smelled like fish, too. He knows what it is like to be human. He loves us anyway, and he calls us to follow him.

Now, choosing to follow Jesus means that we also choose to leave some other things behind. Simon left behind his boat and his nets and the lifestyle he had known before. Jesus may or may not call us to leave our old jobs behind, but he will always call us to leave our devotion to self behind. He calls us to something higher and bigger and better. He calls us to a new life.

That's what baptism is all about. It symbolizes the new life we have with Christ, and the new kind of living he has called us to follow. That new kind of living will always involve loving others and reaching out to them with the hope that Jesus has to offer.

That may change us. It may change us as individuals, and it may change us as a community of faith. That can be scary. Some of us would be a lot more comfortable just staying in the boat or keeping to the shallow water. This business of launching out into the deep and casting our nets into the dark and uncertain waters tends to threaten our nice warm sense of complacency. Do you think Jesus would be satisfied if we just worked hard to maintain our boat and keep it in good order? If everyone said, "My, what an attractive and well-kept boat that is"? Do we really have to go fishing for other people, too?

Yes. Jesus calls us to get out in the deep water and fish, even if it takes us out of our comfort zone and changes us, even if it changes the character of our congregation. Indeed, one could argue that there is no way we can serve God faithfully and stay the same at the same time. Not as individuals. Not as a church. We can't just focus on ourselves and remain faithful. We can't stay on shore. Can't stay in the shallow water. Can't keep our hands inside the boat. Jesus calls us to launch into deep water and cast our nets for a catch.

Are we willing to do what it takes to follow Jesus, or would we rather keep everything the same and stay in the shade? It may seem unpleasant to some, but the truth is that there is no discipleship without change and risk and work and sometimes, perhaps, even smelling like fish.

A WOMAN, A WELL,
AND A JUG

John 4:4-42

*An ancient jug, perhaps perched on a pulpit or a bench,
speaks deliberately but plainly, with the kind of scratchy voice
one might expect from well-worn pottery.*

THE WELL

You may never have heard an old water jar talk before. In fact, I suspect there's a good chance of that. But I hope you'll be patient enough to hear some things I'd like to tell you. I may be made from clay, but so are you, if you think about it, and we're both full of water. When you get down to the heart of the matter, you as children of Eve and I as a worn-down jug have a lot in common.

A lot in common, except that I don't usually get to say anything. It will probably help if you forget what you can see at the moment and picture me sitting on the edge of a well—not a well that's hidden under a big plastic rock with a whining pump attached, or even one with a little well-house and windlass and bucket. No, this well was just a vertical shaft dug straight into the ground, with a row or two of flat stones set around it to protect the opening, and a bigger one to cover the opening when no one was using it. You don't want children or small animals falling into a well: they stink up the water something terrible.

It was a good well, a deep one, a well that could be trusted for water that was fresh and cool. It was an old well, too, one whose reputation went back to the great Jacob himself, one whose stones were worn smooth with long use and grooved deeply by countless draw-ropes.

When you imagine that well, you have to picture it nestled in a handsome valley between Mt. Ebal and Mt. Gerizim. It was deep in the heart of Samaritan territory, in a place where you rarely met anyone but a Samaritan or a Roman. Good Jews of the first century, as you probably know, considered the Samaritans to be right trashy people. Some of the Samaritans' ancestors had been Israelites who were too poor or too unimportant for the Assyrians to carry them off into exile, so they stayed behind. The Assyrians resettled people from other nations they had conquered in the same area, and in time, the Israelites who had been left behind intermingled and intermarried with people from places like Hamath and Luash and Bit Agusi. They didn't forget the God of Israel, but they developed some different ideas about religion that they put into a revised version of the Torah, and they built their own temple on the top of Mt. Gerizim.

When the Jewish people returned from exile, they despised the Samaritans as half-breeds who didn't follow the law. And, for their part, the Samaritans resented the return of the uppity Jews, and didn't make life easy for them. That is why, by the time of Jesus, no good Jew would set foot in a Samaritan town or even speak to a Samaritan, and certainly not to a woman. Good Jews would never come to this Samaritan town, not even for all the water in Jacob's well. The thought of drinking after a Samaritan was enough to turn anybody's stomach.

But the water was still good. In fact, if you didn't care who else had been drinking from it, it was a well that was well worth walking for, even if you were known as a trashy woman who was so unpopular with the other women that you had to let them go first every morning and wait until the heat of the day to draw water so you could avoid their taunts.

THE WOMAN

One day, a traveling teacher named Yeshua decided to take a shortcut through Samaria. I think you folks pronounce his name "Jesus," so I'll do the same. Anyway, Jesus had been walking for a long time, and he was tired and dry. He came here to this well and sat on the ground and leaned back against the stones and took his sandals off even though this low-life Samaritan woman was standing right there beside him. Of course, she wasn't just standing in the sun because she liked to sweat: she had tied a rope around my neck and lowered me into the well. Slowly, quietly, she pulled me back to the top, heavy with water, lifting me carefully out of the well so that I didn't bang against the rocks hard enough to break.

The woman was just untying the rope and getting ready to carry me back home when the man spoke, and she almost dropped me right there on the ground. People rarely spoke to her, you see, not even the other Samaritans. At least, they never spoke kindly. She heard a lot of crude and vulgar comments aimed in her direction, but pleasant conversation was not a part of her daily routine.

That's why she was so shocked when this man spoke warmly to her. There was nothing in his voice that sounded ugly or menacing or controlling. There was nothing in his tone that suggested he was talking to a dog. There was nothing in his eyes that suggested he was looking down his nose. In fact, he was looking up from the ground with eyes like a big puppy when he said, "Would you give me a drink?"

The woman looked around to see who else he might be talking to, but there was no one else in sight. "Would you give me a drink?" he repeated.

Without letting her guard down, she said "*Me?* You talkin' to *me?* You, Mr. Jew, Mr. Superior, Mr. Big Man, you talkin' to me, little Miss Samaritan, and a woman, no less? You been in the sun too long or somethin'?"

The man didn't get up, but the look in his eyes did sharpen a bit. "If you had any idea who you're talking to," he said, "if you knew who it is that just asked you for a drink, and if you had any concept of the goodness of God, then you would ask him, and he would give to you *living* water."

"Well," she said, "Mr. No-Bucket, this is a deep well, and you don't have anything to draw with, so where you gonna find that living water? This well right here was good enough for Father Jacob and his family and his flocks. You think you're better than him or somethin'?"

The man just pointed at me, sitting there with water still dripping onto the stone wall. "It doesn't matter who you are," he said. "Anybody who drinks this water will enjoy it, but they'll be thirsty again. Listen, the water I can give becomes an internal spring that gushes up to provide constant life—*eternal* life!"

The woman just smiled like she thought he was one thong short of a sandal, and she said, "*Sure*, Mr. Magic Man. You just give me some of that everlastin' water, 'cause I'm gettin' awful tired of trekkin' out here in the heat of the day to draw this well water."

It didn't seem to trouble Jesus that she kept missing the metaphor. He knew that she had no way of knowing who he was, out here in the boonies, in a culture of her own. Maybe that was why he decided to flash a little foreknowledge to help her see that he was more than some sun-struck desert hobo. "I'd like to tell you more," he said, with the hint of a wink. "Go get your husband, and bring him back with you, so I can tell you together."

He said that knowing what her response would be: "So who says I'm even married? I've got no husband."

That's when the traveler grinned big and said, "I'll say! You go through husbands like you go through water. What is it, *five* you've had already? I'll bet you've had that old water jar longer than you've had most of your husbands. And at the moment you're living with a man that you didn't even bother to marry, right? So you don't have a husband . . . at least *that* much of what you said is true!"

Now it was the woman's turn to flop to the ground. She almost fainted, but caught herself on her knees. With her mouth, she said "Excuse my tongue, sir, you must be a real prophet!"

But I've been around long enough to know what she was really thinking: "This is getting entirely too personal. Let's see if I can change the subject to something safer, like theology."

So, instead of running to get her nonexistent husband, the woman tried to engage Jesus in a theological debate. "Mr. Prophet, maybe you can explain somethin' to me. Our people have always worshiped here on Mt. Gerizim, but you Jews say that God only listens in Jerusalem. What do you think of that?" (v. 20)

I think Jesus might have enjoyed knowing that his answer would confuse her even more. "Here's what *I* think," he said, "and you can believe it, too. The time is coming when you won't worship either here *or* there, not in any physical place, but in spirit and truth."

"Well," she said. "I don't know about all that stuff. All I know is that we'll get the real truth when Messiah comes—right?"

And the man said, "Yes, I am!"

The woman didn't get it, so she tried again. "I said, we'll get the real truth when *Messiah* comes."

"*Yes*, I am."

"When *Messiah* comes—"

"*Yes, I am!*"

And then it dawned on her. The veil began to lift. She had been met—met by the eternal "I am that I am." Even her Samaritan Bible contained that name. Messiah had come.

And do you know what she did? She left. She ran back into town, yelling at the top of her voice, telling everybody in earshot that she had met a man who told her everything she ever did.

She became, as far as this jug knows, the first woman preacher in Samaria. She went off to tell people about Jesus and bring them out to meet him.

THE WAY

In the process, she did something you may not have noticed, but I did. I couldn't help but notice: what she did was *leave me behind*, sittin' here on the edge of this well.

Sometimes, to do what God calls you to do, to follow the way Jesus puts before you, you have to leave some things behind. Maybe even familiar things you have depended on, things that have brought you security.

I'm just an old jug—I can't claim to know what you might need to leave behind in your personal lives, or in your lives together. What I know is that the woman who once owned me understood that the new joy she found in Jesus made other things seem unimportant. If she thought of me at all, it would have been to realize that she couldn't get back into town with the good news nearly as fast if she was loaded down with a jug full of water.

The woman did not have all her questions answered that day. She did not become an overnight theological whiz kid. But she learned what she needed to know. She learned that there was a word for the emptiness she had felt inside for so long, that yearning she had tried to fill with a string of husbands and affairs. The word was "*thirst*," and she came to know that she was dying of it. But even as she learned to name her thirst, Jesus introduced her to the source of the only water that could quench it, the very Spirit of God, the deep well of life itself.

You never know when you might run across a well like that, for just as surely as your faith becomes comfortable and you think you've got this religion business figured out, you get met. Someone comes along or something happens and God grabs the handle of your heart and points you toward the next stage of your spiritual journey.

You may have noticed that Jesus never did get the water he asked for, but the woman who left me at the well got much more than she ever bargained for. What might God want you to leave behind today? And what is it that he has in store for you? If you but ask, Jesus said, the water of life—in fact, a deep spring-fed well of water—can fill your soul, both now and forever.

Are you thirsty?

Part 4:
PECULIAR TREASURES

MARY AND THE MARCH-ANGEL

Luke 1:26-38; 2:8-20

A Christmas pageant script for a church with a sense of humor. All such pageants involve imagination, especially those that imagine the wise men showed up anywhere near the night of Jesus' birth.

Setting: Mary is alone on stage (except for the baby, of course), sitting by the manger, with a huge star hanging behind. Mary is surprised when the star begins to speak—with a deep Southern accent.

Star: Man, are my wings tired!

Mary: *(startled)* Who's there?

Star: Oh, it's just me, Bubba the March-angel. I'm about to get tired of hovering and keeping up this star disguise. I didn't mean to disturb you.

Mary: *(incredulously)* Excuse me, but did you say *Bubba the March-angel?*

Star: Yeah, that's my name. No need to wear it out.

Mary: You don't sound much like an angel to me.

Star: *(in a mocking tone) You don't sound like an angel to me.* I guess that's why the boss tells me to hang like a star and

	gives all the good lines to Gabriel and Michael. They are *so* proper.
Mary:	You mean . . . you're not all the same?
Star:	All the same? Do you mean angels? Of course we're not all the same. What a boring place heaven would be if all the angels were the same! Of course, you can only be *so* different if you want to have much of a career in the Angel Corps—you can ask old Lucifer about that. But there's room for all kinds of angels! If we're gonna make people welcome from all over the place, then we need different kinds of angels to help them feel at home.
Mary:	What do you mean?
Star:	Well, you've got your dignified ambassadorial angel types like Gabriel, you've got your international angels that come in different colors and speak different languages, you've got your Yankee angels and Southern angels, your uptown angels and redneck angels . . .
Mary:	*Redneck angels?*
Star:	Sure, why not? There's a lot of folks out there from hick towns like Nazareth and Shiloh, and they're gonna need somebody to help them feel down home.
Mary:	I'm almost afraid to ask, but how can you tell if an angel is a redneck angel?
Star:	Oh, it's not so hard. There are several things you can look for. For example, if you see an angel who has numbers painted on his wings and sponsor decals on his chest, he might be a redneck angel.
Mary:	Okay. Anything else?
Star:	Oh, yeah! If you run into an angel who thinks "Amazing Grace" is a waitress over in Jericho, he could be a redneck angel. Or if you meet an angel who thinks the best place to eat in heaven is a little hamburger joint called "The Holy Cow," he might be a redneck angel. Or if you meet an angel who wears a John Deere cap under his halo, he is likely to be a redneck angel. But that's not the easiest way to tell.

Mary: And what would that be?

Star: Well, if you run into an angel with a puffy cheek who sprays tobacco juice every time he says, "Praise the Lord," you're probably looking at a redneck angel.

Mary: Well, Bubba the March-angel, are *you* a redneck angel?

Star: No, of course not! I never owned a pickup truck or a gun rack or a dog in my life. I don't have enough experience to be a redneck angel. I'm just a plain old Southern angel with a plain old Southern name.

Mary: What do you mean when you say your name is "Bubba the *March-angel?*"

Star: You've heard of *archangels*, haven't you?

Mary: Of course I have.

Star: Well, there are a few angels that are really big dogs. Uriel, Raphael, Gabriel, Michael. They're the archangels. And when they tell the rest of us to march, we march. So we're called the march-angels.

Mary: So, Bubba, what do you do when you're marching around?

Star: We praise God, mostly, and believe it or not, there is work to do in heaven. Everything we do is a way of praising the One who made us all.

Mary: So you don't spend a lot of time here on earth?

Star: What? Hang around dirt city when you can cruise the golden streets? Not on your life! Unless the boss gives us an assignment like "Go deliver this message to Zechariah" or "Go and have a talk with Abraham about his nephew." The word "angel" means "messenger," you know. Only occasionally do we get the odd order like "Go act like a star and hang out over a manger in Bethlehem."

Mary: You mean, you aren't assigned to follow people around and watch over them as guardian angels?

Star: *Guardian angels?* Where did you hear that? If angels were guarding everybody, do you think this world would be in the shape it's in? Don't blame that on the angels! Every time you turn around down here, something terrible happens or somebody hurts somebody else. Do you think we'd let that happen if we were assigned the task of keeping you safe? Of course not!

I'm sorry, Mary, but this whole business about guardian angels is just superstition and wishful thinking. People like the idea that they've got angels looking over their shoulder to keep 'em safe, but you can see that it's not true. Nobody is perfectly safe in this world, and it's not our job to keep them safe.

Look—if humans had *angels* running their lives and keeping them out of trouble, they wouldn't be humans anymore. The boss granted humans free choice, Mary. That's a wonderful gift, and you wouldn't be human without it. As much as we might like to step in and change things sometimes, we can't do it. It would violate your humanity. The chief won't let us do that.

Mary: But I thought God sent his angels to help people in need!

Star: Yes, *sometimes* that happens. But it's not automatic. There are some few occasions when the boss, for his own reasons, will send one of us to go and work a miracle in someone's behalf. It can happen, but not enough that you can expect an angelic rescue from every bad spot you get in. That doesn't mean God is not with you in your troubles—it just means you can't expect him to save you from every trouble. Even God has trouble, Mary.

We angels, now, our main job is to be messengers, not world-changers. We can't even be people-changers—but, Mary, did you know? That's why I'm here tonight! The world needs a people-changer. The world needs someone to throw open the door between heaven and earth so everyone can know what it means that the Lord is with them. That someone is your son, Mary. For all this hanging out in a star disguise, I wouldn't have missed this night for anything.

Mary: What do you mean, "That someone is your son?"

Star: I know you've been wondering, Mary, pondering all these things in your heart. I know that Gabriel talked to you some time ago. Surely you haven't forgotten that! And I heard the shepherds tell you what they heard the angels sing out in the fields. The Heavenly Tabernacle Choir doesn't come sing in a shepherd's field just every day, you know. Something very special happened here tonight. Something life-changing. People-changing. World-changing.

Mary: Can you tell me more?

Star: I can help you remember more, and maybe to put things together. Do you remember what Gabriel told you when he appeared that first night?

Mary: He scared me so badly that it's a wonder I remember anything, but every word is still clear to me. "Greetings, favored one, the Lord is with you," he said.

Star: And what do you think he meant by that?

Mary: I don't know. I supposed it meant God had shown his favor on me for some reason.

Star: Indeed he did. His grace is overflowing toward you, Mary. He chose you to be the mother of his own incarnation in this baby Jesus. Do you remember why he told you to name him that?

Mary: The angel said, "He will be great, and will be called the Son of the Most High, and the Lord God will give to him the throne of his ancestor David. He will reign over the house of Jacob forever, and of his kingdom there will be no end."

Star: Amen! And did you ask him to explain what he meant by that?

Mary: No, I asked him to explain how I could conceive a child and remain a virgin at the same time.

Star: I guess that *was* confusing, wasn't it? And it's natural that you'd want to know more about an unnatural thing. But you already recognized those words he was saying, didn't you? The part about how your son would be called the Son of the Most High, and how he would rule over the house of David forever. You had heard those words before

	when the scroll of Isaiah was read, hadn't you? Who did you think they were talking about?
Mary:	Well, the Messiah, of course.
Star:	Of course. The Messiah. The one who would save Israel. And what does the name "Jesus" mean, Mary?
Mary:	It means "salvation."
Star:	So it does. And how do you think the Messiah will bring salvation?
Mary:	I always thought the Messiah would raise an army and save Israel from those nasty Romans.
Star:	Yes, and most other Israelites think the same thing. But what did the herald angel tell your husband Joseph about the child's name?
Mary:	He said, "You shall call his name Jesus, for he shall save his people from their sins."
Star:	Ah! *Sins!* And there's a lot of difference between saving people from Romans and saving them from their sins, isn't there?
Mary:	I guess—I'm not sure what it means to save someone from their sins.
Star:	Well, I can help there, a little. You see, the Lord wants everyone to live in fellowship with him, but sin sets up a roadblock to that relationship. Your child Jesus has come to break through that blockade of sin. In his life, he will teach people how to live in fellowship with God. In his death, he will teach them how to be forgiven and show them God's amazing grace.
Mary:	*In his death? What do you mean?*
Star:	That's all I can tell you, Mary. It's all you need to know. This child's mission will extend far beyond your influence, and his Heavenly Father will teach him what he needs to know about the future. For now, it is up to you to teach him about love, and trust, and hope. It is up to you to bring him up in such a way that when the Father speaks within him, he will listen.
Mary:	I think that is too much for me.

Star: And so would anyone who is worthy of the call. Mary, it is your smallness that makes it possible for you to do big things. It is your humility that allows God to make you great. Never forget what Gabriel first told you—"Greetings, favored one! The Lord is with you." The Lord is still with you now, Mary, and always will be. He will provide the strength you need, and the wisdom, and the grace for every day.

He has given you the most important task in all the world, Mary—to share your love with a child. Love the Lord and love this child with all your heart and all you have, Mary. That is something no angel or star could do.

Mary: I am still the Lord's servant. I will do the best I can.

Star: I know you will. It's late, little mama, and you need to rest. Know that the Lord is with you—and through your son, he is with us all. Good night, Mary.

Mary: *(settling into the hay and smiling)* Good night, Bubba. March in peace!

A SOLDIER'S SOLILOQUY

Matthew 2:1-12

(An interactive drama that reflects on the Christmas story in creative and sometimes humorous fashion, though it deals with a serious subject. Imagine Gomer Pyle and Sergeant Carter of the old Gomer Pyle, USMC *television show as Roman soldiers.)*

Setting: Somewhere near Jerusalem, 2 to 4 BC. Two Roman soldiers in full dress uniform enter (to the theme music from *Gomer Pyle*), a sergeant and a private. The sergeant is distinguished by a fancier uniform, shinier breastplate, or plumed helmet. The audience represents a new class of recruits.

Sergeant: *(speaking to congregation)* All right, recruits. Welcome to Camp Lejunius. I am Sergeant Vincus Carterius, and this is my assistant Private Pylates.

Pylates: *(waving)* Howdy!

Sergeant: I'll be your best friend for the next six weeks. If you survive, you can proudly call yourself a member of the mighty Roman legions. Now, on your feet—let's see if you can march in place. Left foot first. I'll sing out, and you sing back. Got it? *(Pylates helps encourage audience to stand*

and march in place while echoing the sergeant's singsong cadence.)

Sergeant: Left, left, left right left . . .

Audience: Left, left, left right left.

Sergeant: I don't know, but I've been told . . .

Audience: I don't know, but I've been told . . .

Sergeant: King Herod's got a pot of gold.

Audience: King Herod's got a pot of gold.

Sergeant: I don't know but I hear tell . . .

Audience: I don't know but I hear tell . . .

Sergeant: he pays his soldiers very well.

Audience: he pays his soldiers very well.

Sergeant: He's looking for some men like you . . .

Audience: He's looking for some men like you . . .

Sergeant: and maybe even women, too.

Audience: and maybe even women, too.

Sergeant: Sign up today and you will see . . .

Audience: Sign up today and you will see . . .

Sergeant: how great it is to be like me.

Audience: how great it is to be like me.

Sergeant: Sound off . . .

Audience: Sound off . . .

Sergeant: Sound off . . .

Audience: Sound off . . .

Sergeant: Sound off 1, 2, 3, 4—sound off!

Audience: Sound off 1,2, 3, 4—sound off!

Pylates: Sergeant? Sergeant?

Sergeant: What is it, Pylates?

Pylates: Gorlee, Sergeant *(brandishing clipboard)*, is this where I'm supposed to start writin' their names down?

Sergeant: I'm coming to that, Private. Just keep your shirt on.

Pylates: Shazzam, Sergeant! My mama told me not to never take my shirt off in mixed company!

Sergeant: As I was saying, recruits, if you don't turn out to be the weakest links, you might be able to join the main corps of Caesar's finest fighters. If not, goodbye!

Pylates: Yeah, goodbye!

Sergeant: Stuff it, Pylates!

Pylates: Sergeant? Don't forget to tell them about the secret code for meal call: that's real important for new recruits!

Sergeant: Okay, Pylates, why don't you just tell them about that.

Pylates: Well, when it's time to eat the mess—it's not really mess but that's just what we call it—you'll know it's time when you hear the secret code.

Sergeant: And what is that code, Pylates?

Pylates: Hooty hoot! Hooty hoot!

Sergeant: Thank you, Private. You got that right the first time.

Pylates: Surprise! Surprise!

Sergeant: One day you might just make a good soldier, Pylates.

Pylates: Thankee thankee, Sergeant!

Sergeant: Now, listen up, recruits, this is a crucial time, and we need some good people for assignment here in Palestine. The Jews are making noises about revolution, and their King Herod is very sick.

Pylates: Oh, gorsh, Sergeant, how sick is he?

Sergeant: He's very sick, Pylates. So sick that they say his flesh is rotting off his bones. But it's not just his bones that I'm worried about, Pylates.

Pylates: What do you mean, Sergeant?

Sergeant: What I mean, Private, is that King Herod has some "psychological issues."

Pylates: He has what?

Sergeant: You know, he's one camel short of a caravan.

Pylates: Huh?

Sergeant: He's nuts, Pylates! Can't you understand plain Latin? The old coot is so paranoid that he's been having his own wives and children killed, because he thinks they were plotting to take his throne.

Pylates: Oh, gorsh, Sergeant. How could he do a thing like that? I don't care if he does have "issues." Shame, shame, shame is what I say! How long has he been like that?

Sergeant: Well, I have my own ideas about that. He was always a suspicious sort, but he really started going downhill after those three wise guys from the East showed up.

Pylates: You mean the ones that came in with all the camels and jewels and stuff? The ones that talked so funny and said they were lookin' for a baby?

Sergeant: Those are the ones, Pylates. They showed up one night and said they were looking for the new king. That really set old Herod off! He called for his guards and had those dudes at spearpoint before you could say "Bluebird Café." They yanked on their beards and hollered for diplomatic immunity, but he didn't care.

Now Herod got it out of them that the guys were royal astrologers from some eastern country. They had seen a new star over in our direction and figured that it must be the sign of a new king. They had copies of the Jewish holy books, and they had found where some prophet named Micah had said a new ruler would come out of Bethlehem.

You know that's the last thing Herod wanted to hear, but he figured he would let these traveling wise men find the young pretender for him, so he made them promise to come back and tell him where they found the kid. Herod made like he wanted to come and give honor to the future king, too, but we all knew what he really wanted. *(draws finger across throat, like a knife)*

The wise guys were smart enough to see through Herod's game, so they promised to come back, but never did. I'm sure they tipped off the kid's parents, too. That's when Herod really lost it, Pylates. He went red in the face and ordered us to kill every boy baby in Bethlehem from two years old and down. It was the ugliest, most awful thing I'd ever seen. There weren't more than a couple of dozen boys that age in Bethlehem, but that was too many. I shudder to remember it . . . all those innocent little guys

. . . all that blood . . . my hands will never be clean again, Pylates.

But they didn't get the one they were after. I know it in my gut. I've known it ever since that night two years before when the skies lit up and those shepherds went bonkers.

Pylates: What do you mean, Sergeant?

Sergeant: My platoon was doing security detail in Bethlehem during the census, Pylates, remember that? And we really needed it. You've never seen such a crowd: so many of these Jews claim to be descended from David, and they all had to be counted in Bethlehem because that was David's hometown.

I pulled the night shift, and late that night, out over the shepherd's fields, the whole sky lit up for a little while, and there was a noise like thunder. We went out to investigate, and ran across a group of shepherds that were babbling like madmen. "The sky was filled with angels!" they said. "The angels proclaimed that a savior had been born in the city of David," they said. They kept muttering something under their breaths that we couldn't make out. "Immanuel, Immanuel!" they said.

We got a translator over and figured out that was Hebrew for "God with us." We interrogated the simpletons for a while, but it was no use. They all kept babbling and stuck to the same story. So we just trailed them into town and hunkered down. They went down to a stable behind old Lumas's inn. Sure enough, there was a baby down there. Newborn, too. But his folks were obviously peasants, really poor. They couldn't possibly be a threat to Herod, and we couldn't possibly explain all those lights in the sky, so we just kept quiet, but I always wondered . . .

Pylates: Wondered what, Sergeant?

Sergeant: I always wondered what was so special about that baby that a whole flock of angels would show up to announce his birth. You see, I believed the shepherds, Pylates. I've been keeping an eye out ever since. Somehow I have the feeling that I might just meet him again someday, some way, somehow. Maybe you will, too, Pylates.

Maybe you will, too, recruits—but I don't know what to tell you to look for. Some guy named "Immanuel," I guess. Just keep your eyes open . . . you never know when he might show up, or what he'll be doing, or what he might ask of you, or what you'll be called to do. Just, be ready. Be ready.

Take their names, private.

THE MEN IN THE PEN

By Dr. Leuss

Acts 5:27-32

*Imagine how Luke's story about Peter and John's imprison-
ment would have sounded if it had been translated by the
inimitable Dr. Seuss. With a tip of the hat to the cat . . .*

THE MEN IN THE PEN

The sun did not shine in our jail cell that day.
The walls were all cold and damp and gray.

I sat there with Peter. We sat there, we two.
With our heads stuck in stocks, there was little to do.

So all we could do was to sit, sit, sit, sit!
And we did not like it down there in the pit.

All we had done was to preach the good news
and to heal a few people, both Gentiles and Jews,

But the high priest was angry—the Sadducees were mad!
So they put us in prison for what we had said.

It was late in the night and we'd been there all day
when Peter suggested that we ought to pray.

So we prayed through the evening and into the night,
In hopes that our God would show us some light . . .

And then something went "Bump!"
How that bump made us jump!

We looked! And we saw him step in with a nod,
We looked! And we saw him—the angel of God!
And he said to us, "Why are you looking so odd?

"I know it seems bleak while you're here in the lurch,
but God isn't finished with you or his church!

"So I've come with a message that's plain and that's simple—
God says to go back and to preach at the temple!"

And Peter and I did not know what to say,
but we knew it was better for us to obey.

So the angel reached down and he unstuck our stocks,
then he turned to the door and he unlocked the locks.

While all of the guards and the prisoners slept
we snuck out of that place where the crooks were kept.

We went back to the temple in the dark of the night,
then we started to preach at the morning's first light.

We said, "Look at us! Look at us! Look at us now!
We're back out of jail! Do you want to know how?

"Our God came to save us! He helped us! It's true!
And I'll bet if you open your heart he'll save *you*!

"God has a plan for your days full of strife—
Jesus has come to give you new life!

"The same one you saw die his death on a hill—
He rose up again and he's living still!"

And many there were who believed us that day,
but soon the armed guards came to take us away.

The priest said, "No! No! Tell those Christians to quit!"
For they did not like us, not one little bit.

So they dragged us to court and gave orders to us,
Said, "We told you to stop and we told you to hush!

"Your preaching is planned to make us look bad
and blame us because your Jesus is dead!"

But Peter just said, "We don't care what you say!
It's not other people, but *God* we obey!

"It's true that you killed our teacher and Lord,
but God raised him up and God gave us this word!

"You cursed him and nailed him to your ugly tree,
But God will forgive even your cruelty.

"We know what we're talking about, don't you see?
He's already forgiven my friend John and me."

Then the high priest called out all the Sadducees
and they wanted to kill both Peter and me,

but a Pharisee stood, named Gamaliel,
a man who had lots of respect, you could tell.

He said, "If these men are just spreading a lie,
then leave them alone and their movement will die.

"But if they are truthful, although it sounds odd,
Do you want to find yourselves fighting with God?"

So they beat us and told us to preach no more
unless we liked that jailhouse floor,

but Jesus had called us to tell the good news,
so we left there and did what he told us to do.

Now, what would *you* do if your Master told you?

The Church in the Lurch

What *would* you do, if your Master told you? That's not a rhetorical question, you know. When we come to the end of Dr. Seuss's *The Cat in the Hat*, and we read the closing question, "What would you do if your Mother asked you?" we don't really have to answer, because we have not really been visited by the Cat in the Hat.

But when we read Dr. Luke's story in the book of Acts, and it challenges us to ask ourselves what we would do, we have to answer the question. The God on the Cross *has* visited us. He has offered us forgiveness of sins and a new kind of life. He has called us to a life of service in which we learn to obey God rather than any human authority or human influence.

We who live in America are rarely troubled by that first part. We live in a land where we are free to express our faith and to worship without fear of reprisal. But it's really not the human authority that matters when the question arises as to whom we will obey.

There is another kind of influence or authority at work that is more pervasive and also more persuasive than any government regulations. It is the force of our culture, our society's expectations, the pressure of our peer group.

Are we afraid to talk about our faith for fear that our friends will not understand, and so we keep quiet, with our tongues locked in the stocks of timidity?

Are we afraid to be different from the rest of our society, for fear that we will be ostracized?

Are we afraid to tell our children the truth about what our culture has done to Halloween and Christmas and Easter because we are more influenced by commercialism and culture than by our Christian faith?

Are we afraid to live a simpler life that allows us to be more generous in our support of Christian ministries and more able to help the poor because our culture demands that we become slaves to bigger mortgages and higher car payments and more credit card bills?

This story of Peter and John setting an example and standing strong despite opposition makes a powerful claim on our lives. It is a powerful story because it declares the truth of the gospel. No more than a week before this story took place, Jesus' disciples were defeated and disheartened and hiding out for fear of their lives.

But then something happened to change all of that: Jesus rose from the dead, just as he said. Jesus rose from the dead, and his resurrection had such a powerful effect on those early believers that they came out of hiding and began to preach the good news in every corner of the city with no fear, even when the religious authorities arrested them and beat them and threatened to kill them.

Why would they dare to do this? Because they believed it was really true. That Jesus truly lived and reigned. They came to believe there really was a hope for an abundant life and an eternal life. They came to feel the reality of Christ's Spirit living and active and working within them to bring blessings to the lives of others.

Since they earnestly believed these things, and they really wanted to be a part of God's kingdom, there was little choice to be made: they would obey God, rather than any human authority. They would obey God, even if they took a beating for it, even if they were put in jail because of it, even if they were killed for daring to be different.

It is tempting, even as a church, to focus on pleasing ourselves and pleasing our culture with little thought for pleasing God. We want to make everybody happy, to provide a building and an atmosphere that will make everybody comfortable, and to be good neighbors in our community so everyone will be glad to have us around.

But it should not be the church's first intention to make its membership happy.

It should not be the church's first intention to make its community happy.

It should not be the church's first intention to make its staff happy.

It should not be the church's first intention to make its youth happy, or its children, or its preschoolers.

It should not be the church's first intention to make the choir happy.

It *should* be the church's first intention to make *God* happy. And what pleases God is a faithful people who are true to their God-given mission.

That was Peter's first intention, and John's, and Paul's. That is why we are called to stand with Peter and declare, "We must obey God rather than any human authority"—even when that human authority is our own opinions or desires.

Is it time to put the right intentions into our personal lives and our church lives before our materialistic culture steals us blind and leaves us with only an empty shell?

Peter said, "We must obey God rather than any human authority." What do *you* say?

WEIRD JOHN AND THE GOSPEL OF CHANGE

Matthew 3:1-17

This could be presented as a monologue by someone in costume, or read offstage in a darkened room while the congregation views a slide of a ruggedly portrayed John the Baptist. John speaks in a rather gruff, countrified voice, with an attitude.

I see you staring, so we might as well get on past the fact that I don't look like you. I don't look like most preachers you've seen, either. In fact, except for a little foam around the mouth every now and then, I probably don't look like *any* preacher you've ever seen.

Now get this: *I don't care.* If you think I look like a madman, the only thing I care about is this: *"Made you look!"*

That's because you need to look, and you need to listen. I've got a message for you that people have been ignoring for hundreds of years, and it's about time somebody paid attention.

Now, some of you observant types out there may be wondering why I chose this get-up to get your attention. It's not the only option. I could have worn clown shoes and a big red nose, couldn't I? I could be wearing a space suit, or I could have dressed like the Grim Reaper. That would get your attention, wouldn't it?

It might get your attention, but it wouldn't tell you anything about who I am, would it? I'm not a clown or an astronaut or an angel of death. I'm here as a messenger of life, and if you've paid any attention at all to the Holy Scriptures, you'll know who I am because there aren't many prophets around who look like me. In fact, there's only been one other.

Do you remember that old story about King Ahaziah of Israel? Now there was a hopeless case if you ever saw one. He had this nice patio room up on the flat roof of his palace in Samaria, up where the cooler air moves and the mountain views are nice. The room was mostly made of windows covered with thin latticework that gave some privacy but still let the breeze blow through and provide some relief from the heat. One day the dolt was trying to get cool, and he leaned on the lattice and broke right through it. Ahaziah fell straight off the edge of the palace and got himself broken up really bad.

Now, here's the amazing thing, even though this king's name meant something like "Yahweh has held on," this king was not holding on to Yahweh, to the Lord. He thought he was going to die from his injuries, but did he pray to Yahweh? No! Instead, he sent messengers to a pagan temple way down in Ekron to inquire of the god Baal-Zebub whether he would live or not. Now, I ask you, how was a piece of gold-plated wood supposed to know anything?

Along the way, this old prophet of Yahweh who was always tellin' people to repent intercepted the messengers. He knew what had happened, and jumped out in front of them and pointed his finger and said, "You go tell that worthless king that *I* said, 'Is there no god in Israel, so that you have to consult Baal-Zebub? Don't expect to be gettin' better, you worthless pagan. You're a dead man!'"

Well, they ran and told King Ahaziah what the old prophet had said, and when the king heard it, he asked the messenger, "What did this man look like who told you this?" And the messenger said, "Well, he didn't give his name, but he was some kind of strange looking. He was really hairy and all he had on was a piece of animal hide around his waist."

And the king said, *"That's Elijah!"* (2 Kgs 1:1-8).

Of course it was Elijah. Do you know what Elijah's name means? *"My God is Yahweh!"* That's our Hebrew name for God, you know. *Yahweh.* There's power in a name like that.

Elijah's name meant "My God is Yahweh," and he lived like it—unlike King Ahaziah, who denied his name and didn't hold on to Yahweh, but served other gods.

Elijah was some piece of work: if you ever met him, you never forgot him. He spent a lot of his time in the wilderness. He didn't wear a lot of clothes other than that piece of animal skin around his waist, and he ate whatever the land provided. He looked like a wild man and some people thought he was touched in the head.

He was touched, all right, but touched by God.

There's something else that's rather interesting about Elijah. Do you remember what it was? The old codger didn't die. You won't find any bones from the prophet Elijah, because one day he just turned the job over to his associate Elisha and hopped on a fiery chariot that swung down low and picked him up and carried him home (2 Kgs 2).

You can imagine that people thereabouts had something to say about that. In time, what they started to say was that Elijah had unfinished business to do, and that he would come back one day. Do any of you people remember the very last verse in the very last prophetic book of the Hebrew Bible?

No? I didn't think so.

So I'll tell you. The last words of the book you call the "Old Testament" were written by the prophet Malachi, and this is what he said: "See, I will send you the prophet Elijah before that great and dreadful day of the Lord comes. He will turn the hearts of the fathers to their children, and the hearts of the children to their fathers; or else I will come and strike the land with a curse" (Mal 4:5-6, NIV).

I'll bet you never thought about that . . . the last prophetic words in the Old Testament are a big *"Or else!"* It's a prediction that Elijah the prophet would return, and that he would call the people of God to repent and turn back to God before the last day, and they would either listen and change—*or else* the land would be struck with a curse.

Nobody wanted to be cursed. What they wanted was somebody to put the promise back in the "Promised Land," so people were on the lookout for Elijah's return, and many of them were primed to hear his message and turn back to God.

And then, 200 years later, I showed up . . . and what did I do?

That's right—I lived in the wilderness. I wore camel hair and a leather belt. I lived on locusts and wild honey most of the time, and I had one sermon that I preached again and again: "Repent, for the kingdom of heaven is near" (Matt 3:1).

Sound familiar? Makes you wonder, doesn't it? My parents didn't name me Elijah—they named me *Yohanan*, which you pronounce as "John." *Yohanan* means something like "Yahweh is gracious." Yahweh was gracious enough to keep his promises and send a word of warning to his people.

Now, I know what you're thinking: did I come as the actual reincarnation of Elijah, or just as one in the spirit of Elijah? I'm not telling, but it doesn't matter. What matters is the message, and my message was this: "Repent, for the kingdom of heaven is near."

People remembered what old Malachi had said about Elijah coming back, and thousands of them came out to the wilderness to hear me preach. Some of them had also remembered the prophet Isaiah, and that he once declared a day would come when people would hear a voice calling from the desert, shouting, "Prepare the way for the Lord, make straight paths for him!" (Matt 3:3).

And there was a lot of straightening that needed doing, let me tell you. There was a lot of crookedness going on in Israel, and it's not hard to see there's a lot of crookedness in your world, too.

I called on people to turn their lives around, to leave their crookedness behind and to straighten up. That's what it means to *repent*, you know. It means *to change*. People would come up and say they wanted to repent, and I would tell them if they were serious about changing their lives to just come on down in the River Jordan and let me dip them in the water to show everybody else they were planning to leave crookedness behind.

Hundreds of people came out there and lined up for me to baptize their crooked selves in the river, but I wasn't convinced that some of them were ready to straighten up. Some of those people were self-righteous sorts who were really as crooked as snakes, and I've never been afraid to call a snake a snake, so I said, "Who sent you out here, you sons of serpents? Who warned you to run from the judgment that's coming?" (Matt 3:7).

"I know what you think," I told them. "You think you've got it made because you can trace your family tree all the way back to Abraham, but I'll tell you what: that pure pedigree of yours don't mean a thing if your life doesn't match it! God can raise up children of Abraham from these muddy stones on the riverbank if he wants to. If you want to take the plunge and get straight with God, you've got to prove that you've left your squirming, snaky ways behind: you've got to bear some fruit that demonstrates your repentance!

"And I'll tell you what: there's an ax whistling through the air right this minute. It's looking for trees that use up the land but don't bear any fruit, and when it finds them, it's going to chop them to the ground, and they'll be thrown in the fire! [based on Matt 3:8-10].

"The times are changing," I told them. "You don't get any credit for who your ancestors are or what your parents did. You've got your own roots, your own limbs, your own leaves. What I want to know is, have you got any fruit?

"I ask, because you need to know something. You might think I'm something out of the ordinary because I dip you in this water, but I'm telling you that somebody is on his way who is so special that I can't hold a candle to him. I'm not worthy to carry his sandals. I baptize you in this water, but he's going to wash over you with the Holy Spirit and with *fire!*

"Did you hear me? He's coming like the master of the harvest, and he's coming to the threshing floor looking for good grain, and all that chaff that looks like grain but isn't—that's going to the fire!" (from Matt 3:11-13).

Some of them listened, but a lot of them just put their noses in the air and took down the names of the ones in the river.

But while they were taking names, I saw something that took my breath. I saw my cousin Jesus come walking down into the water, and all of a sudden, my heart did a flip, and something inside told me he was the one I'd been talking about. My name might mean "Yahweh is gracious," but *his* name means "Yahweh *saves!*" While I was fulfilling

Isaiah's prophecy about preparing the way for God's salvation, he was the one who'd be walking down it.

Jesus came wading up like he wanted me to baptize him, but all I wanted was be baptized by him. I wanted to be baptized with that Holy Spirit and fire I'd been talking about. But he wouldn't have it that way. Seems like he wanted to identify with all those crooked people around him, or maybe to set a good example for them, I don't know, but anyhow he said, "This is the way it needs to be, John—dip me." And who was I to argue with him?

So I dipped him the same way I did everybody else, and that's when all heaven broke loose. That Spirit of God I'd been talking about came down with such force and power that you could *see* it, and it lit on him like a dove on the branch of an olive tree, and I could hear a voice that confirmed in my ears what I already knew in my heart, because it said, "This is my Son, the Beloved, with whom I am well pleased" (from Matt 3:14-17).

And when Jesus went off and started preaching on his own, do you know what he said? "Repent, for the kingdom of heaven has come near" (Matt 4:17).

It was the same sermon I'd been preaching, but he had much better illustrations than I did, and a lot more spirit and power to back them up.

I kept sounding off for a while, but I told any disciples I had to follow Jesus, and it wasn't long before I wound up in jail anyway. That old fox who calls himself "King" Herod didn't like what I had to say about him marrying his brother's wife, and she liked it even less, so we got into a rather heated discussion about it. You could say, in fact, that I really lost my head.

In any case, I needed to clear out and leave the way open for Jesus. That, after all, was my job. It was his job to take the hard road from there to Calvary.

It's a crooked world we live in, but that doesn't mean we have to live crooked lives. We can change. That's what repentance is all about. You may not believe it, but you can change. Life can change. Change is possible, change that is for the better, change that is ongoing.

We don't have to stay as we are, where we are. We can turn from our crookedness and follow Jesus down that road that leads from strife and death to peace and life. We can trust his guidance to help us make a better life, not only for ourselves, but for others.

We can . . . yes, we can.

What about it?

SUGGESTED TOPICS, SEASONAL USAGE

INDEX BY SCRIPTURE